Fact
and
Fiction

in
The Da Vinci Code

Fact
and
Fiction

in

The Da Vinci Code

Steve Kellmeyer

Bridegroom Press   Peoria, IL

Copyright 2004 by Steve Kellmeyer

ISBN:0-9718128-6-1

Printed in the U.S.A.
Bridegroom Press
PO Box 96
Peoria, IL 61650
www.bridegroompress.com
E-mail: info@bridegroompress.com
Phone : 309-685-4085

Contents

INTRODUCTION

He has always been the source of controversy. That's why the man got crucified, after all: people disagreed about who he was and what he intended to do. The solution to the disagreement was fairly straightforward – general experience tells us that if you kill the person who is bothering you, he tends to stop bothering you. Most days of the week, that's sufficient. After all, violence really *does* solve a lot of problems. True, it tends to create new problems, but the old ones are solved. In cases like Jesus, the dead man soon fades away into memory and then becomes even less than memory. He is at best a strange tale in an old man's doddering dream, or a one-sentence footnote in a pedant's scholarly paper.

That was the plan. But plans rarely survive contact with the enemy. This one certainly didn't. You see, his disciples insisted he rose from the dead. That created problems.

To begin with, the story was plausible. After all, his execution was quite public, as was the spear-thrust into his side that confirmed his death. He was laid in a tomb hewn out of solid rock and sealed with another solid rock – no tunneling was possible. It was guarded by soldiers, indeed, by the very men who had killed him. These soldiers were in turn ruled by a governor who would execute them without a thought if they failed in their guard duty. His followers were cowards – they had run like rabbits the minute he was arrested. There was no way on God's green earth that this particular corpse could disappear.

But it did.

The whole thing was quite puzzling. His disciples didn't move the corpse – they were still cowering in some corner or other, certainly no match for the guard. The soldiers who killed him certainly didn't move it. Neither did the small group of men who agitated for his death. Yet the stone was moved; the tomb was empty.

And things rapidly got worse. His followers, craven, yellow-bellied, uneducated, stupid fishermen that they were, had suddenly acquired backbone from somewhere. Serious backbone. The authorities couldn't get them to shut up, even after a public whipping and a lot of jail time. Or, at least, it was meant to be a lot of jail time. The impertinent jackasses kept getting out somehow – no one knew how. Pilate might have allowed the leader to be executed, but with this rabble he really did wash his hands.

And the worst of it was, they kept proclaiming this Jesus was actually alive. Stupid men. They didn't deny that he had been crucified and killed, they *emphasized* it. They said he rose from the dead. Indeed, one of them insisted he even probed the dead man's wounds with his own fingers. And they weren't alone. The whole populace had seen the brutal scourging and crucifixion Jesus had died from, they all saw the brutal scourging his loud-mouthed rabble-rousing followers took, they saw this uneducated riff-raff dragged off to prison but none of it kept others from insisting they had seen Jesus too. In fact, Jesus was appearing to all of the people he had once eaten and drunk with, upwards of 500 people at a time.

It was most unsettling. The rabble-rousers were explaining Scripture to the crowds as if they were teachers of the Law. Where on earth did they get such knowledge? None of them had studied with a teacher. True, they had been with that Jesus for a couple of years, but he had had no formal training in Scripture either. Of course, everyone admitted he had been rather good at explaining Holy Writ– even the most learned men couldn't seem to out-think him. But his followers had all been stupid as rocks. Their dimwitted responses to Jesus' teaching was legendary – some of the scribes still laughed at the idiocy they showed while their leader lived.

But the jokes were few and far between now. These peasant fishermen dared to pretend that all the prophecies of Scripture were fulfilled now in him. Worse, they were convincing hundreds, thousands, of this every day. And they had somehow become just as slippery in debate as their dead leader had been. The change was amazing. In the space of seven weeks, they had been transformed from uneducated cowards into intellects of frightening power and even more frightening courage. Some of the Jews they confused with their words could be bullied and badgered out of this absurd belief, but there was a core group of leaders, about a dozen men, that simply couldn't be touched. These men even had the chutzpah to stand on Solomon's Portico and preach this fulfillment of prophecy. None of the scribes, the Pharisees, the Sadducees – not one had the guts to stand them down anymore.

How *did* they keep getting out of prison?

Where *did* they get their sudden backbone transplant?

But most of all, where did they get that *teaching*?

And where *did* his corpse go? No one could find it – and believe me, they looked.

And so it went. Some suggested that the Romans had gotten the wrong man, but the eyewitnesses to the event, including the men who conspired to kill him, knew that wasn't true. The Romans had gotten the right man – everyone had seen to that.

Some claimed he didn't die. That was preposterous, of course. The Romans might be ignorant when it came to the Torah, but they were masters when it came to execution. Even if they had somehow absurdly failed to kill him, how was a man who had taken a Roman scourging and crucifixion supposed to move that rock and battle through all those trained soldiers? Without a tool to his name or a weapon in his hands? No, that was silly.

Men began to group themselves according to the different theories put forward. The Cerinthians and Ebionites both insisted Jesus was just a man, not God, but they couldn't agree on how that worked. The Nicolatians said Jesus was God and sin was now impossible, so they lived lives of unrestrained indulgence. The

Docetists said Jesus was God but had never actually had a body – the crucifixion, his life on earth, all of it was an elaborate divine illusion, which is why his body couldn't be found. The Gnostics said there were actually two gods: the evil god of the Old Testament, called the Demiurge (he created the world in order to trap human souls into the prison of material reality) and the good and kind Propater, who sent Christ to tell us how to get past the Demiurge.

The Christians insisted he was God and God had taken on flesh. The core group of men, who called themselves apostles, insisted that anyone washed in the name of the Father, the Son and the Holy Spirit would be divinized. God possessed the one divine nature, they said, but every baptized individual shared in the divine nature. This grace gave a person the power to live as Jesus lived. And they proved it.

You see, years became decades, decades became centuries, centuries became millenia. Time after time, different theories were put forward, different contentions made, all of them designed to refute these "apostles" and their silly ideas about Jesus and divinization. But all of these theories and contentions shattered on the hard facts.

The corpse that couldn't disappear *had* disappeared without a trace. No one came up with a satisfactory explanation except the apostles and their successors.

The apostles, famous cowards and idiots, were suddenly the shrewdest, most courageous men the world had ever seen. All but one of them were brutally tortured to death in order to force them to admit that Jesus was not God: not one of them broke. In this, their deaths were uncannily like their leader. The one who did not die from the torture - his name was John, and everyone agreed he was the disciple most beloved by Jesus - was boiled in oil, but it affected him no more than a warm bath on a cold spring day.

Worse, the same could be said for pretty much everyone who had followed Jesus. Many were bullied, badgered, even tortured. Nearly to a man (or even woman, even children), they wouldn't change their minds even to save their lives. It was the most astonishing thing.

But worst of all, the teaching they brought forward *did* explain the prophecies of Scripture in the most coherent way anyone had ever seen. You just had to believe one incredible, impossible, absolutely absurd thing:

Jesus really rose from the dead.

If you accepted that single event as fact, everything else made sense. If you rejected that single event as falsehood, then you had your pick of theories. None of them worked very well.

We are about to see why.

Welcome to a page-by-page analysis of *The Da Vinci Code*.

STRUCTURE OF THE BOOK

This book is designed to follow the structure of the novel as closely as possible. Each section lists the subject addressed, in addition to the chapter and page number of *The Da Vinci Code* on which the relevant discussion in the novel can be found. As a result, discussions of some subjects are split over several individual sections. Where possible, these split discussions refer the reader to the other sections that discuss the same or similar topics. This format makes it much easier for those familiar with the book to find the specific topic they desire. As in the original book, the initial chapter commentaries are foundational to understanding many of the later discussions, thus the discussions should be read in order whenever possible.

One other thing should also be kept in mind, an idea best explained through an example. In 1905, the Russian secret police released an earth-shattering document. According to this document, a secret meeting of Jewish leaders had assembled in order to discuss their plans to establish a world government and persecute Christians unremittingly. The document contained the notes from this meeting. Leading figures around Europe were shocked at the revelations. Anti-Semitic pogroms against the Jews followed quickly on the heels of the document's publication.

By 1920, this document, *The Protocols of the Elders of Zion*, was shown to be an anti-Semitic forgery. Despite this, Henry Ford continued to promote the work throughout the United States until 1927. It also formed an important part of the justification for Nazi policy in Germany. Indeed, *The Protocols* are still widely accepted as true in many parts of the world.

Whenever we encounter a work of historical fiction, it pays to keep *The Protocols* in mind. The reason is obvious: it is easy to start confusing fact and fiction, and that can lead to dangerously mistaken understandings of the truth.

Like many other excellent pieces of historical fiction, *The Da Vinci Code* must be approached with care. Since the jacket cover and the book's literary category acknowledges that it is a work of fiction, we know much of what it presents will not be true. On the other hand, the very first page of the work claims "All descriptions of artwork, architecture, documents, and secret rituals in this novel are accurate." Thus, we know Dan Brown wrote what is often called an "alternate universe" history: a history of what the world might look like if a single historical event had turned out differently.

Many authors have done this with marvelously intriguing results. What might have happened if Germany won World War II? What might have happened if the difference engine, also called the computer, had become popular one hundred years earlier than it did? Dan Brown asks a similar question: what might the world look like if the Catholic Faith were founded on a lie? What if Jesus was not God, but just a married man like anybody else?

The question is obviously popular: his novel was on the bestseller's lists for quite some time. In this work, we will examine the assertions made in the novel and demonstrate where Mr. Brown hews close to historical fact and where he is obviously spoofing historical knowledge.This work addresses the vast majority of assertions made by the characters in the novel. Enjoy.

FACT

PAGE 1

Mr. Brown begins building his "alternate universe" history right from the first page. His statement is exceedingly clever. Clearly, presenting a series of facts is not the same as providing an accurate interpretation of the facts presented. Yet, by wording it in this way, Mr. Brown encourages us suspend disbelief and explore a mythical universe of his invention. His sleight of hand in this opening page helps us forget that interpretation of facts makes all the difference.

For example, if Mr. Brown had decided to write an alternate universe story concerning former President Bill Clinton, he would have an ample set of facts to draw upon:

- The Democratic party was the party of the American slave-owner through the 1800's.
- While Republicans always opposed slavery, Democrats long fought to maintain its existence.
- The Ku Klux Klan is pro-slavery, anti-Catholic and has secret rituals.
- The Arkansas chapter of the Ku Klux Klan is the largest and most active Klan chapter in operation today.
- Bill Clinton was born and raised in Arkansas, it is also where he attained political power and prominence.
- Though it is true that prior to the Civil War some Catholic priests in Arkansas violated Catholic teaching by supporting slavery, the priests and members of Opus Dei have always followed the eternal teaching of the Catholic Church in opposing slavery.

So, using these facts, Mr. Brown could easily write a stirring thriller based on the secret rituals of the Ku Klux Klan and descriptions of actual geographical locations in Arkansas and Washington D.C. He could use the artistic power of the pro-Klan movie *Birth of a Nation* and the stirring eloquence of Mr. Clinton's addresses. Combining facts about art, architecture, documents and secret rites, he could compose a novel in which Bill Clinton, the sitting Democratic president, attempts to institute a legal sex slave trade in the United States, and is kept from doing so only by the last-minute heroic actions of Opus Dei. If he were to write such a novel, he could easily make a statement identical to that which begins the *Da Vinci Code*. Indeed, this is, quite possibly, the story line of his next novel. Though his facts are accurate, it is his interpretation and arrangement of the facts that creates the "alternate universe."

But the dry facts may not be enough to be fully convincing. Perhaps the book would work better if some of the facts are massaged a bit. It is not difficult to do. After all, who really remembers all the stuff we were supposed to learn in school? At most, we remember words, phrases, but never their context and often we don't remember even the facts themselves. For instance, we might dimly remember a "Whiskey Rebellion," but where, why and who fought are probably long gone from our minds. So, by massaging the content of the Whiskey Rebellion, Dan Brown can easily turn the event into something that supports the plot line of his next novel: *Monica Unchained.* Keeping this in mind, let's begin our exploration.

"PAIN IS GOOD"

PROLOGUE, PAGE 5

Silas, the Catholic layperson who dresses like a monk for no apparent reason, mouths these words in the prologue of the book. This is our first clue that we are dealing with an "alternate universe" story. No well-taught Christian would say such a thing. It is a heresy. Pain is a natural evil and morally neutral. C.S. Lewis' excellent little book, *The Problem of Pain*, goes into more detail than is possible here, but we will address the subject very quickly.

A natural evil is something that was not originally part of God's design for the world. God created everything good. Pain, at least to the extent it is present today, is not part of God's original design for the world.

Now, there is a difference between natural evil and moral evil. Natural evil is a result that man created for himself, it is not what God intends for man. Hurricanes, tornadoes, blindness, plague, physical or mental deformity: these are all natural evils. How can man cause hurricanes? We have to understand how the world works.

Grace is power. It is the power that keeps the universe running harmoniously. God set mankind up as stewards who care for the world. God sends grace into the world. We are supposed to direct it so as to help all creation bring greater glory to God.

When God sends grace into the world, man has two choices. He can accept the grace God sends new every morning, or he can reject it. If mankind rejects grace, then the world does not have the power needed to work harmoniously. We are all acquainted with machinery that breaks when it is run with insufficient power. The world is exactly that kind of machine. When we choose to reject the power of grace, the world inevitably fractures. Natural evils such as those listed above are some of the fractures.

As stated above, there is a difference between moral good/ evil and natural good/evil. Morality refers to the consequences that are visited on persons. A morally good act fills a person with grace. A morally evil act strips grace away from that person. Each person can only affect his own state of grace. I cannot strip grace from you, nor can you strip grace from me. Conversely, I cannot add grace to you, nor can you add grace to me.

A natural good or natural evil refers to a created thing that is not a person. If a created thing is working the way God intended it to work, it is a natural good. If it is not working the way God intended it to work, it is a natural evil. Natural goods and natural evils also have no effect on persons. A natural good will not add grace to a person, nor will a natural evil remove grace from a person.

However, when created things work the way they are supposed to, we generally find it easier to act in a morally good way. When created things do not work the way they are supposed to, that is, when we encounter a natural evil like plague or drought or physical deformity, we tend to find it more difficult to act in a morally good way.

Now, earlier we noted that no human person can add to or injure another person's state of grace. However, we *can* each add to or strip away the grace in a situation. This is a poor example, but it will have to do: suppose I see you sitting in front of a malfunctioning computer. I fix the computer. I have "graced" that situation, because I have turned a natural evil (your broken computer) into a natural good through the skills that grace has bestowed on me. As a result, your ability to retain the grace you have is much improved.

On the other hand, if you were sitting in front of a working computer and I harmed it or harmed you (perhaps blinding you with acid), I have used the skills given me by grace in order to strip away grace from the natural objects around you. Now you are forced to deal with natural evils, a situation that shouldn't be the way it is. As a result, you are much less likely to be able to hold onto your own grace. For my part, I have misused the grace within me, and I am now emptied of it. Grace is power precisely because it is the presence of God, and God will not abide in one who does evil.

How we respond to the natural goods and evils we meet every day influences how we decide to cooperate with the grace that dwells within us. The idea is this: no matter what comes our way, we will choose to cooperate with the grace, the power, within us, we will not choose to empty ourselves of it in despair.

When we take something good and grace-filled – the human act of sex, for instance – and intentionally empty it of grace, we simultaneously empty ourselves of grace. But God sends grace new every morning. When we use the grace He sends to fill and thereby heal a situation that lacks grace, the very act can open us up so that God can fill us with even more grace if He chooses.

God is the source of grace. We experience pain because the world is short on grace. If the world is the road to heaven, pain is one of the potholes, a possible impediment to reaching our destination if we hit it wrong and/or use it wrong. However, if at the moment we encounter pain, we remain open to the God Who is the source of grace, we become a pipeline. If we cooperate with the grace He places within us, He can use us as instruments to fill the potholes in the road. The world's pain is lessened. Not only do we find ourselves on the road to heaven, but we have also helped make the road smoother for others to follow. Thus, like an athlete training for a marathon, a Christian can say "pain is good" only in reference to the pain he himself endures as part of the work he does with God as God goes about healing the world.

So, in the context given by Brown, Silas' statement is absurd. Silas just shot a man and he's telling his victim pain is good? Silas knows full well his opponent doesn't understand the reason for pain nor does he understand how to use the pain inflicted on him. This injury is not good for that man or for anyone else.

There are only two possibilities: either the thing the museum curator is hiding is true or it is false. If it is true, God cannot be harmed by it, for God is Truth. If it is false, God cannot be harmed by it either, because God's Truth is stronger than any falsehood. Shooting the museum curator is completely immoral, a purely evil act that strips grace from the situation by inflicting a natural evil, and strips grace from Silas, who has performed a morally evil act. See also "Holy sins & absolution through sacrifice," Chapter 2, page 13 "Christianity: man-creator, woman-sinner," Chapter 56, page 238.

PAGAN SYMBOLISM IN CHARTRES CATHEDRAL
CHAPTER 1, PAGE 7

Here is our second clue that Dan Brown is using an "alternate universe" form of historical fiction. Do such pagan symbols in Chartres exist? It is impossible to tell, since no further information is provided. Even if it were true, however, such a thing would obviously not ruffle Catholic feathers, conservative or orthodox. After all, it is perfectly in accord with Scripture.

Judeo-Christian Scriptures acknowledge that God, by definition, can use anything the created universe contains in order to accomplish His purpose. That's what it means to be God, after all. Thus, the Old Testament is rich with examples of pagans who inadvertently did precisely what God wanted, even though these same pagans thought they were simply following their own desires: Pharoah or Cyrus are excellent examples. Likewise, Paul did not hesitate to explain how the pagan "idol to an unknown God" was actually devoted to Christ (Acts 17:22-31), nor did he hesitate to use two lines from pagan poets to show how Christ's presence is evident in the life of every person, believer or non-believer (Acts 17:28).

It isn't hard to see why this would be so. We are all born pagans. Through baptism, God changes who we are, incorporating each baptized person into His own body. We are God's co-creators. If God can baptize us and bring us to full participation in worship of Him, then we can "baptize" the physical instruments we use, that is, our tools can also be used as a way of giving glory to God. We fell away from God, God turns us back towards Him in baptism. Because we are stewards of the universe, the universe also fell away from God in the Fall. God can also turn the universe back towards Him.

The word "revelation" means "to pull back the veil." Historically, God has used three means to reveal Himself to us: the natural world, the prophets, and His own Incarnation.

Every faith tradition recognizes that God reveals Himself through the evidence of the natural world. Although the various traditions may argue about *what* the natural world proves, none argue that the natural world constitutes proof about the ultimate reality who is God. This is primarily where the problem of evil arrives, because the natural world inflicts both good and evil upon its inhabitants. Every branch of human knowledge, religious or secular, is essentially an attempt to provide a coherent explanation for why this happens.

Note that virtually all religions share broad agreement on what constitutes good and what constitutes evil. It is generally agreed that stealing is wrong, lying is wrong, murder is wrong, etc. The murderous Thugee cult of Kali or the Aztec practice of human sacrifice might be pointed to as exceptions here, but even in these instances, human sacrifice was generally not seen as a good in itself, but an evil that had to be tolerated in order to prevent a greater evil - the destruction of the world, or a similarly cataclysmic event.

The very fact of this general agreement shows that Someone has instilled in us concepts of good and evil. There is coherent, visible, proven structure to the universe. All of Western science is based on this concept: the idea that objective reality exists and can be discovered, investigated. Indeed, historians of science generally agree that this concept is exclusive to the Judeo/Christian worldview. No other philosophical system has a clear beginning and a deterministic endpoint. Since all the other philosophical systems are cyclic, they prevented the rise of a coherent scientific worldview and the rise of science itself. Although a specific philosophy might make specific progress in a specific area (like Chinese gunpowder), none made the broad progress in several areas simultaneously that those based in Christian philosophy did. This proof of the presence of divinity provided by the natural world is called "natural revelation."

Likewise, the revelations of the prophets provide us with unique understanding of God. Again, virtually every system of belief has someone who acted as a prophet: Plato for the Greeks, Buddha for Buddhism, Manes for Manicheans. The Greeks considered anyone highly intelligent to have a share in the divine mind. Buddha refused the idea that he was God, but insisted that the eight-fold path led to enlightenment. The examples could be multiplied. We are most familiar with the prophets of the Hebrew Scriptures and the apostles of the Church. The witness of prophets is also a form of divine revelation. Prophets tell us quite a lot more about God than nature does, but they still don't tell us enough.

God knows this, so, the Creator speaks to us directly. This is the only method not present in all belief systems. Buddhism doesn't have it in the Western sense of the term because it is not monotheistic in the Western sense, still, the very idea of entering into No-Mind or Nirvana gives a dim sense of the idea. In Hebrew Scripture, it is much more clear. God speaks directly to man on a regular basis. For Christians, of course, God actually takes on human flesh in order to make the message perfectly clear. Dan Brown provides an echo of the Judeo-Christian understanding in the very last lines of his book.

These are the three ways we can know about the Creator: natural revelation, and the two forms of personal revelation, prophets and direct communication from the Creator Himself. Clearly, not every form of communication gives the same amount of information. The less information one has, the more likely it is to be corrupted or misunderstood in some way. Thus, while pagan religions that have only nature to rely on will get some part of God's communication right, other parts will accidentally be misunderstood or misrepresented. The pagans simply don't have enough information. After all, the natural world does not provide enough context. Ask any scientist. The book of the world is pretty confusing at times.

So, it is perfectly reasonable to find that pagans have discerned some truths about God. It would be decidedly odd if they did not. Likewise, it is perfectly reasonable for Christians to present those truths that pagans have. Truth is truth, no matter who first recognized it. Pagan symbols are generally very crude attempts to give glory to God. Why re-invent the wheel? People who have been given a clearer communication will naturally streamline the very crude forms, make them more clear, more capable of giving God even greater glory. The authors of the Old Testament did it, so did the apostles in the New Testament. There is no reason to exclude accurate representations of the truth, even if they are crude because they were first brought forward prior to the fullness of revelation God directly gave us Himself.

HOLY SINS & ABSOLUTION THROUGH SACRIFICE
CHAPTER 2, PAGE 13

We already know Silas is an absolutely abysmal Catholic, a murderer and a heretic. Now we begin to discover the depths of his misunderstanding of Catholic Faith.

Absolution is the forgiveness of sin. Absolution is given and sin is forgiven through the sacrament of confession, not through whipping yourself until you bleed. A sinner's experience of pain does not get rid of sin, and no Christian has ever taught that it does. If any Christian did, he would be condemned as a heretic. Us sinners are the ones blowing holes in the world, the road to heaven. It would be surprising if we did not feel pain, both from our own sins and from the damage inflicted by the sinners around us. But a sinner is not open to God's grace, he has no way of healing the world or himself. Instead, he has rejected the power necessary to heal the situation. Grace is the power of God's presence, but God will respect our wishes. He won't enter where He is not wanted.

So, only someone who already bears grace within himself, that is, only someone who is innocent, and who is willing to stand in the midst of the fractured world's pain, bearing God's presence into the midst of the fractures, only such a person can bring the necessary work of healing. That is the only pain that can bring wholeness. There has only ever been one completely innocent man, and He is the only one who was able to stand still and bear the world's burden while the grace poured in and did the healing.

The pain of Jesus Christ crucified is the only pain that is able to expiate the sins of the world. He chose to stand in the dyke and turn back the flood of pain, thus all the power necessary to heal the wounds of the world flowed in. But there is still a problem.

The grace to heal the world is now available, but one thing is still required. Each of us has to accept that power into our own lives, each minute of the day. Christ's Cross does not take away our ability to choose. At every moment, we each can accept or refuse the grace He won for the world. Every time we refuse it, we re-injure the world, we re-introduce pain, both for ourselves and for others. In that moment, I plunge myself back into the predicament the whole world suffered before healed it. What to do?

The sacrament of confession is the way a sinner bloodlessly, painlessly joins himself to Christ's sacrifice, and has grace restored to him. This sacrament of reconciliation is where Christ on the Cross forgives the sinner for what the sinner has done to the world. Silas is, to put it mildly, extremely confused on this point.

But that's not the worst of the mistakes Silas makes in this page. He muses on "holy sin." There is no such thing as a holy sin. God's presence is grace, it is power. Holiness is the presence of grace. Sin is the absence of grace. These things are opposites. The idea of "holy sin" is a self-contradiction. Anyone who speaks in this way doesn't understand the first thing about God. Silas is not the only character in the book who strings words together in such a way that the result is meaningless or self-contradictory, but he's certainly the character who does it most often. See also "Christianity: man-creator, woman-sinner, Chapter 56, page 238."

Fighting God's enemies assures forgiveness
Chapter 2, page 13

The set of statements found here is close enough to sound dimly factual, even though it isn't. As was noted earlier, only a direct appeal to Jesus Christ in the sacrament of confession He established assures forgiveness. In fact, the way the earliest Christian soldiers "fought" for the Faith was by accepting martyrdom. The early Church is filled with soldier-martyrs who were killed by their commanders for being Catholic.

Arguably, no one fought for the Faith through actual combat until perhaps the 700's, when Charlemagne attempted to subjugate the Germanic tribes. Even that is being generous: part of his rationale may have been dressed in religious terms, but his warfare certainly had a lot more to do with the politics and economics of keeping his kingdom safe from barbarian assault.

The next best candidate for acts of war against God's enemies are the crusades, which started in the eleventh century. Still, even that occurred only after six hundred years of constant provocation by Muslims. The armies of Islam had taken over the entire southern half of the Christian Roman Empire by 732 A.D. By the mid-800's, Muslims routinely enslaved Christian children throughout their territory, often brutally castrating them. By 1009 A.D., they had destroyed the holiest site in Christendom, the Church of the Holy Sepulchre, which had been erected over the tomb of the risen Christ. About the same time, they also cut off access to the Holy Land. Meanwhile, their armies advanced inexorably in the East, threatening to overwhelm the Christians in Constantinople.

Despite five centuries of provocation, the Catholic Church did nothing. The Pope only declared Crusade after the Christian emperor of Constantinople, his front lines overrun by the armies of Islam, pleaded for assistance from the West. During the actual waging of the wars, the Crusaders never targeted the holy sites of Islam for destruction. They stopped when they got Jerusalem back.

This explains the difference between the Christian concept of "just war" and the Muslim concept of "holy war." As can be seen from the example of the Crusades, just war is based on principles of self-defense. Just as a woman has a right to fight off a rapist, so a nation or state has a right to fight off an aggressor. In order for war to be just, several principles have to be adhered to: (1) the war must be waged to protect innocents from unjust attack or rank injustice and it must intend to restore peace; retribution is not a just cause, (2) it has to be waged by competent authority – rulers who oppress their own people can be justly subjected to revolution, (3) all other non-violent means of redressing the wrong must have been exhausted, (4) there must be reasonable hope of success, (5) the method of waging war must be in proportion to the wrong it is redressing, (6) it must do more good than harm and (7) non-combatants may not be targeted.

Muslim "jihad" operates according to principles at once similar and different. While jihad must use proportionate response, must avoid injuring non-combatants, and must cease if the enemy sues for peace, it is based in a right to proselytize. Islam claims a right to evangelize that leaves its opponents only three choices: accept

Islam themselves, permit it to be preached so others might accept it, or permit it to rule their lives. If all three of these options are rejected, then Islam is permitted to wage war and all Muslims are expected to support those who participate in this war.

Jihad assumes a right to proselytize that Christian just war theory does not. That's why Islam besieged Vienna not once but twice in one hundred and fifty years, the last time in 1683, just a century before the American revolution and the Enlightenment. The Christian response, a European army led by the king of Poland, just barely recovered the city and repulsed the Muslim army.

Still, even though Islam menaced Europe through the 1800's, Europeans largely stopped using Christian Faith as a basis for war by the middle 1700's. The reason is simple. It was a lousy rationale for war.

Since the rise of Christendom in the 300's A.D., the most advanced thinkers of Europe spent a millennium developing Christian doctrine and dogma. The very word "theology" is derived from "theo" and "logos" - it literally means "conversation about God." The science of theology was the pre-eminent scientific discipline. Still, though Christian theology abolished the pagan cyclical universe and replaced it with a Christian linear worldview, the science of theology was not itself a natural science.

The systematic study of nature, that is, natural science, didn't really begin until most of the work involved in building a coherent, consistent Christian philosophy had been done. Since Christian philosophy was the only self-consistent philosophical framework Europe had, it is not surprising to see that anyone who wanted to do anything in Europe used this philosophical framework to justify their actions. There wasn't any other system of reason as well-thought out, as robust, as capable, as the philosophy supporting Christian Faith.

But, as the sciences of economics and biology developed through the 1800's, they quickly replaced Christian Faith as the justification for armed conflict. This is not because the 19th century versions of economics or biology were particularly robust or well-thought out. They weren't. But pretty much anything was better at justifying armed conflict than the language of Christian Faith.

Christian philosophy was extremely robust, but it wasn't very martial. Not only did just war theory hobble both intentions and methods, the Church heaped restrictions on when it could be waged. Battles, for instance, generally could not be fought on Sundays or holy days or during the seasons of Advent, Christmas, Lent or Easter. Waging war during harvest was permitted, but not a good idea – the crops would rot in the fields without men to harvest them. These restrictions left very little time for battle. Rulers very much wanted to get rid of the Church's inhibiting rules.

Thus, Christian Faith really didn't support the kinds of mayhem that combatants wanted to engage in. That's why we don't hear any Christian leaders preaching crusade today. Science, especially the sciences of economics and eugenics, is much better at justifying mass slaughter than Christian Faith is. Science lets you fight whenever you want, killing whoever you want in whatever way you want. But the nicest thing about science is that it invents its own tools of mass-destruction to enhance the slaughterhouse experience. So, instead of being limited by what is morally permissible, you are limited only by what is physically possible. When the goal is to see who can pile body bags the highest, there's no contest: nation-states will seek to ground their reasons for war in science every time.

THE RELICS OF WICCA

CHAPTER 4, PAGE 23

Wicca does not have any relics. The Wicca religion was invented during World War II by English civil servant Gerald Gardner (1884-1964). He just slapped together material from a few pieces of fiction and some *really* bad anthropology (a woman named Margaret Murray figures prominently here). Serious historians of Wicca agree that Wicca is no older than most people's grandparents, certainly not old enough to generate relics.

Gardner invented the religion primarily because he liked to walk around in the nude, and Wicca gave him a religious rationale for doing so (an interesting, if unstated, reason for the nude murdered man in the novel). Gardner originally built his slap-dash religion around a single God of Death, but ultimately realized he was more likely to get nude females to participate if he added a goddess. Obviously, this also gave him a chance to commit adultery, since the initiatory rites tended to be sexual in nature (it is unclear how his wife, Donna, reacted to his witch coven activities). Gardner's work is the source of all the goddess religions practiced today. Oddly, while a ritual sex act is described in the book, Langdon fails to describe how Wicca initiates are ritually spanked with a sword. Perhaps describing that would put Wicca ritual too close to the Opus Dei practices of the antagonists.

Incidentally, Robert Langdon is at pains to point out that Wicca has nothing to do with satanism. Wicca is based on Gardner's work. Gardner stole ideas from Margaret Murray, who, in turn, stole from Jules Michelet's *La Sorciere* (available today under the title *Sorcery and Witchcraft*), a 19th-century work of literary Satanism. In short, Langdon doesn't appear to know much about the origins of Wicca, which is indeed grounded in satanism.

DESCRIPTION OF ROBERT LANGDON

CHAPTER 4, PAGE 24

Eighty percent of books sold in America are sold to women. Mr. Brown is not only a good novelist, but a smart man, very good at manipulating his plots. His protagonist is a woman's dream, a handsome, sexy man complete with an irrational fear of small spaces that just gives a girl a reason to hold him close. Indeed, the whole plot is meant to appeal to the twenty-first-century post-Christian woman. This is yet another clue that Dan Brown is writing a specific kind of "alternate universe" history.

OPUS DEI

CHAPTER 5, PAGE 29

To Mr. Brown's credit, he gives a very nice two paragraph defense of Opus Dei on this page. Unfortunately, he follows that defense with a 400 page series of unsavory Opus Dei caricatures. By the end of the book, Bishop Aringarosa will turn out to be a fideist heretic, and Silas will have indulged in several more heretical or plain silly pseudo-Catholic acts. If Opus Dei routinely produced people like this, the Pope would be perfectly justified in suppressing the organization. Fortunately, this version of Opus Dei exists only in the "alternate universe" of *The Da Vinci Code.*

"Opus Dei is... a Catholic Church"
Chapter 5, page 29

This demonstrates why the Opus Dei organization described in the book is pure fiction. No bishop in the world would talk like this, certainly no Opus Dei bishop would. A Catholic bishop might say, "We are part of the Catholic Church" or "We are a member of Christ's Church", or "We are an order of the Church" or "We are an organization of the Church" but never "We are a Catholic Church". There is only one Church, so all references to it are preceded by "the", never "a." Phrasing it without the definite article implies that there is more than one Church founded by Christ and that is a heresy. Even heterodox Catholics who embrace extremely problematic teachings avoid this terminology because it is so... well... so *not Catholic*. The reader might encounter a Catholic group called "We Are Church" but will never encounter a Catholic group called "We Are A Church".

The first sentence Bishop Aringarosa speaks in the book is so odd that very few Catholics could read it without stumbling a bit in surprise. Reading the bishop's phrasing is like finding a wild rabbit in your bathtub – you may become accommodated to it eventually, but the first meeting is a bit of a shock.

Devil worship
Chapter 6, pages 35-36

See the discussion of Wicca for chapter 4, page 23.

PAGANS

CHAPTER 6, PAGE 36

Pagans were indeed country folk, and the derivation of pagan and villain is perfectly accurate. However, pagans – by definition – did not worship a single god or goddess. They worshipped darn near anything that came to hand. There was nothing unified about their beliefs or their rituals. But there is a kind of irony in Langdon's commentary.

When we look at the "red counties" versus the "blue counties" in the 2000 Bush-Gore election, it is precisely the Christian "pagans," that is, the Christians who live in rural areas, who voted the Christian George Bush into office. The city atheists voted for Gore. Unlike the ancient Romans, today's pagans *are* pretty unified in their beliefs, and those beliefs are Christian.

Thus, we have a key to discovering where Mr. Brown's "alternate universe" lies. It is interesting to note that Langdon uses exactly the strategy he accuses the Catholic Church of using. That is, Langdon's discussion of paintings and other symbols are worded so as to undermine the faith of Christian rural folk. Throughout the novel, Langdon co-opts Christian symbols: he attaches new meanings to important icons of Christian culture, meanings that simply were never originally present. Thus, what the novel does in this universe is a spiritual version of what the Opus Dei characters do in the novel – kill belief. Mr. Brown neatly identifies his own "alternate universe" as the ideological enemy whose arcanely weird practices are based in falsehoods and should be abolished.

Olympic Games and the Pentacle
Chapter 6, page 36

In this universe, Venus does trace a kind of pentacle in the sky, but it is by no means perfect. The Olympic games were originally held in honor of Zeus, not Venus-Aphrodite. The number of circles in the modern Olympics symbol was supposed to increase after every game, but the organizers stopped after five when they realized that the games were now well-established and any further additions were going to get silly fairly quickly. The dissonance between reality and the novel are made clear by Langdon's silence in regards to a rather important question. If the cycle of games was meant to symbolize a relationship to Venus, why would the games be held every half-cycle, every four years? Wouldn't it make more sense to do it every full cycle, that is, every eight years?

Like many of the other "goddess links", such as the military stars, the stripes on an officer's sleeve, the Disney allusions, etc., the connections being made are clearly part of an "alternate universe" story. In Langdon's fictional universe, Venus *does* make a perfect pentacle, Zeus had nothing to do with the Olympic games, Jesus was married, the Catholic Faith is false. The examples could be multiplied.

Opus Dei's gift to Rome
Chapter 7, page 40

Opus Dei has indeed given millions to Rome. So has the Knights of Columbus. Indeed, so has pretty much every major Catholic organization in existence. All the parishes of the world donate money to the Holy See year after year. One of the duties of every baptized Catholic is to support the Church. And why not? Even the smallest secular organization collects dues and/or accepts gifts.

Similarly, Jose Marie Escriva's cause *was* put on a "fast track" in John Paul II's reign. But *every* canonization process was put on a fast track in this pope's reign. He streamlined the process, got rid of a lot of procedures that used to be required, and encouraged everyone to make public the lives of holy people. As a result, Pope John Paul II has canonized more saints in twenty-five years than the entire Church had in the two millennia preceding him. Think about this for a moment. This one pope has publicly identified more saints than all previous popes combined. In Mr. Brown's "alternate universe," John Paul II has apparently been much less productive. It makes for a better story Mr. Brown's way, but it makes for a better world John Paul II's way.

WOMEN "FORCED TO ENDURE" PRACTICES
CHAPTER 7, PAGE 41

It is worth mentioning that *The Da Vinci Code* makes no mention of organized sports at all. In his alternate universe, football players are not forced to endure hours in the blazing sun, running mindless patterns in the grass, nor are baseball players, soccer players, marathon runners, etc.

Of course, in our world, people join organizations in order to do things that other people would never think of doing. People who have never lifted weights in their life find membership in a health club a perfectly silly idea. Others do this gladly. It all depends on what you think will benefit you.

Wiccans and others involved in goddess worship undoubtedly have rites that others would find strange. Gardner's prediliction for walking around in the nude and committing ritual adultery leaps to mind. In Langdon's universe, the pursuit of mindless pleasure, like adultery or drug addiction, is not addressed. However, consciously permitting some discomfort into your life appears to be "a dangerous practice." No one in his story mentions the "No pain, no gain!" rule. No one in his story pursues excellence in physical endeavors, for that would mean a willing acceptance, even a pursuit, of a certain level of discomfort in their physical lives. Indeed, in this world, people who frequently run for exercise often pursue the "jogger's high," which sounds suspiciously like a semi-spiritual experience. It would provide too jarring a dissonance to the storyline to point out that the Christians described in these paragraphs pursue something along the same lines. But a master story-teller is at work. His idea is to avoid dissonance and keep the reader trapped in the story. See the commentary on "The Chalice and the Blade," Chapter 56, pages 237-239.

LEONARDO'S LIFE AND THE VITRUVIAN MAN
CHAPTER 8, PAGE 45

In Langdon's world, the circle signifies feminine protection, and there is nothing more to discuss. Never mind the box that also encases the figure in Leonardo's drawing. We are supposed to ignore it because it isn't important in Brown's alternate universe.

Langdon's artist is quite a bit different than the Leonardo who inhabited this reality. For instance, in Mr. Brown's world, everyone calls him "da Vinci," while in this world, even the least informed art historian knows that "da Vinci" is merely a reference to his region of origin. His name is Leonardo, and that is what everyone with a background in art calls him. Though charged with sodomy once in his life as a youth, there isn't much evidence he was homosexual, much less a flamboyant homosexual.

He was not a man who produced much artwork. He did not accept "hundreds of lucrative Vatican commissions", in fact, he spent very little time in Rome, got one commission from the Vatican, and never finished it. No one really knows what he believed. He didn't write down much concerning his beliefs on non-art subjects and no one else did either.

THE AMERICAN CATHOLIC CHURCH AND THE

SEX SCANDAL

CHAPTER 8, PAGE 48

In Langdon's world, the Catholic Church in America suffers from a pedophilia scandal. In this reality, of course, the Church in America does not suffer from a pedophilia scandal, it suffers from a homosexual scandal. Practicing homosexuals who also happened to be priests were in the habit of preying on young men, that is, they invited teenage males to have sex. In the vast majority of cases they did not have sex with pre-teens. The priests were not pedophiles - they were simply active homosexual men.

Older homosexual men routinely seek out teenage boys. In fact, it is so common in homosexual culture that older gay men who act this way have a specific nickname: gay men call them "chickenhawks." Thus, the homosexual priests were simply "chickenhawks" doing what any red-blooded homosexual male typically fantasizes about or does. They had sex with pretty teenage boys.

There are three mysteries here: selectivity, culture, and plot. For people who live in our universe, the mystery is media selectivity: why does the media promote the homosexual lifestyle everywhere except when Catholic priests embrace it? The priests' understanding of celibacy was essentially no different than at least one American president's understanding, and he got a pass. Further, why does the media attack the Church for the four percent of her priests who abuse, but ignore public school teachers, given that the American Medical Association reports seventeen percent of boys and eight-two percent of girls are sexually abused by public school teachers and/or staff? Shouldn't the public schools be vilified as well? Since forty percent of public school sexual offenders are repeat offenders who simply get shuffled to another position because of tenure, shouldn't we have grounds for outrage there too? But this is a mystery for our world.

In Langdon's universe, the mystery is slightly different: why is a French detective upset? In our world, the firestorm was an essentially American phenomenon. The Europeans showed little interest. Mr. Brown's French investigator would be an odd duck in our world. Frenchmen have their own problems, and the American scandal isn't one of them.

Finally, a word about plot development. The inspector's comment comes near the beginning of the book. It has nothing to do with the plot, very little to do with character development, it simply appears out of nowhere, then is never mentioned again. A reader who lacks Christian charity might suspect an ulterior motive for mentioning the scandal. Such a suspicious reader might quote Langdon's character, "Misunderstanding breeds distrust" and assert that Dan Brown is just trying to stir up all the negative feelings he can about the Catholic Church, an organization he does not understand. But this kind of suspicion is ridiculous. Mr. Brown would certainly never demean the reader by stooping to such base emotional manipulation. He is above such things.

TAROT CARDS

CHAPTER 9, PAGE 92

In the Catholic Mass, the Latin form of the words of consecration are: *Hoc est enim corpus meum.* It has been said that the popular dance, the Hokey Pokey, was originally intended to mock the Catholic Mass, the genuflection (put your right leg in, put your right leg out), the elevation of the Host, etc. When you hear the full explanation, it sounds very convincing. None of it is true.

Roland Lawrence LaPrise and two fellow musicians created the song shortly after World War II for the ski crowd in Sun Valley, Idaho. The Ram Trio recorded the song in 1949 and Ray Anthony, the bandleader, bought the rights in 1953, in order to make it the B-side of the Bunny Hop. It has nothing to do with an assault on the Catholic Mass.

Similarly, the explanations given for the meaning of the Tarot cards could only be true in an alternate universe, since they aren't true in this one. Tarot cards were developed as a 15th century gambling device. Occultists only began using them in the early 1800's. A great book on these kinds of things is Tom Burnham's *Dictionary of Misinformation.*

EARLY SCIENTISTS

CHAPTER 20, PAGE 94

In our universe, Galileo lived in the late 1500's and early 1600's, and he was the man who first described the scientific method. Science does not exist without the scientific method. Thus, describing anyone prior to Galileo as an "early scientist" is anachronistic, if not downright silly. The Greeks were pretty good philosophers, but pretty lousy natural scientists precisely because they weren't very good at observing nature. They had not the necessary tools, they had not the scientific method. Aristotle is an excellent case in point. His observations were wrong in fundamental ways, and slavish adherence to his theories by both Muslims and medieval Europeans seriously hobbled the development of natural science in both cultures for quite some time. In Langdon's universe, things apparently worked out differently, and science arose much, much earlier than it did here.

This creates certain problems in the plot's context. If science arose earlier in Langdon's universe, that could only happen by the establishment of a philosophy which said the world had a definite beginning and was moving towards a definite end-point. Hinduism, Buddhism and similar cults all share a common characteristic. They all view history as a wheel, a never-ending story where the ending becomes the beginning and the whole thing repeats, endlessly. This idea is also present in goddess philosophy, indeed, it can be seen in the very structure of the *Da Vinci Code* novel itself. The story ends virtually where it begins, with Langdon waking up in the same hotel, thinking the whole episode a dream. In both the beginning and the ending, he goes to the Louvre to find a corpse (the curator and Mary Magdalene). In both the beginning and the ending the dying man is "pallid" and has been shot to death with a wound to the stomach (the curator and Silas). If all novels had to follow this kind of plot, we would stop calling them "thrillers."

Christianity is the only philosophy that ever broke Langdon's "feminine circle." By establishing a definite beginning (creation) and a definite end (the Last Judgement), by asserting that the natural world is built precisely in order to reveal the glory of God, Judeo-Christian faith forced theologians to pursue study of the natural world in order to fully understand who God is. Christian theology requires natural philosophy, which in turn necessarily leads to natural science, which then unlocks the door of technological advancement. In this sense, the Darwinian concept of evolution is not so far from the truth as many Christians might suppose.

The difference between theological inquiry into nature and atheistic inquiry into nature, lies precisely in the difference between a bridegroom on his wedding night and Dr. Frankenstein in his laboratory. The bridegroom sees the bride slowly revealed. Frankenstein also sees the bride, but only after building her. Theology insists that the Divine Spouse already exists in beauty; we need only to wait for the veil to be fully removed. Evolution insists the spouse has to built.

THE NUMBER PHI

CHAPTER 20, PAGE 95

Through this discussion, we discover that Langdon's universe shares many of the same properties as ours. The discussion of phi is largely accurate. However, no one has been able to figure out why it is in the book, except as a way for us to discover that Langdon's universe is physically similar to ours. Despite the last sentence of the discussion, the number might be used to demonstrate divine order, but it certainly doesn't tell us whether God has a sex, or if He does, what sex that is. It has nothing to do with the plot. Perhaps Mr. Brown inserted it in order to help readers suspend belief and give Robert Langdon credibility. It is, after all, just about the only monologue in the book in which Langdon's hypothetical universe does not diverge in a major way from our own.

LEONARDO'S "DOCUMENTED" GODDESS WORSHIP
CHAPTER 20, PAGE 96

See the comments on Chapter 8, page 45. Goddess worshippers don't believe in original sin. For them, Genesis is a patriarchal lie meant to put women in a bad light.

Leonardo, however, did believe in original sin. His proof lay in the fact that friction existed on earth, where Adam and Eve fell and grace was in consequently short supply. But friction did not exist in the heavens, for the heavens were untainted by original sin; there the perfect spheres of heaven moved in frictionless tracks. There is no evidence Leonardo worshipped in a goddess cult, and his statements concerning original sin are strong evidence that he did not.

It would be interesting to discover if Langdon's universe also depicts John F. Kennedy as a lesbian cross-dresser or Bill Clinton as an Ethiopian cattle butcher. Given the lack of documentation in this world for either claim, it seems quite possible that both would be true in Langdon's universe.

THE THREE-FOLD GENUFLECTION
CHAPTER 23, PAGE 107

Catholics genuflect, true, but no Catholic would make a threefold genuflection. It's silly. Ask any practicing Catholic.

THE PRIORY OF SION
CHAPTER 23, PAGE 113

In our world, it certainly exists, but it was only constituted into existence in 1956. Our universe did have an Order of Sion from 1090 to 1188, but it bears no resemblance to the Priory that exists in Langdon's universe, the "oldest known secret society in the world." For us, the intervening history linking the two was totally invented by Pierre Plantard in the late 1960's. Plantard was convicted of crimes involving embezzlement and fraud in 1953. In the 1960's, he created the Priory of Sion legend in an unsuccessful attempt to demonstrate that he was the uncrowned king of France.

Unsatisfied with his first attempt at historical fiction, Plantard created a second account in the 1980's that completely contradicts the first account. Langdon's universe apparently sticks to Plantard's first version, since Langdon's version includes the Knights Templar – Plantard's second version had replaced the Knights with the Children of St. Vincent. Plantard stopped writing histories of the Priory right after a court warned him that if he didn't stop, he would face further jail time. Langdon appears to be completely unaware of this.

This poses one possible problem for Mr. Brown, however. In the prologue to his work, he says, "All descriptions of artwork, architecture, documents, and secret rituals in this novel are accurate." It isn't clear whether he violates this promise or not, since he doesn't tell us whether these "facts" are accurate in his fictional universe or in this one. Certainly there was no chest containing Mary Magdalene's bones and confirming documents in this universe. However, there might have been one in the universe he created.

MONA LISA DISCUSSION
CHAPTER 26, PAGE 119

Mona Lisa was not Leonardo in drag. Contemporary documents in our universe tell us she really existed and sat for the paintings made of her. The anagram wordplay is amusing after the manner of cloud-watching: "Doesn't that cloud look like a duck?" The woman's name was Madonna Lisa. Guess what her nickname was.

MALLEUS MALEFICORUM, HAMMER OF WITCHES
CHAPTER 28, PAGE 125

Langdon's universe diverges sharply from European history here. In his world, the *Malleus Maleficarum* was used by the Catholic Inquisition to kill five million women over the course of three hundred years.

In our universe, life was pretty different. Witch burning was a Renaissance and Early Modern phenomenon, concentrated mostly in Germany, Switzerland and eastern France. By the time it really got going, these areas were dominated by Protestants, not Catholics. Women were not the exclusive targets – nearly 90% of the witches executed in Iceland were men, for instance, while the convicted witches in Russia were predominantly male. Less than 15,000 executions have been documented for the whole of European history. Reasonable historians estimate that less than 40,000 deaths could have taken place. This accords with common sense: if five million women had died, Europe would have become a depopulated wasteland long before the three centuries were up. Women *do* tend to have the children, after all.

While the *Malleus* was written by an Inquisitional judge, it was never used by the Catholic Inquisitional courts because it was judged absurd. In fact, one of the authors, Heinrich Kramer, was censured shortly after its publication. Only secular courts used the *Malleus*. Indeed, the two countries with the strongest religious court systems, the Catholic Inquisitional courts of Spain and Italy, also had the lowest number of witch trials and executions. While Pope Innocent VIII did issue a bull permitting the Inquisition to search for witches in 1484, Catholic doctrine generally held that the whole witchcraft craze was a product of wild imaginations. Inquisitional judges stopped several instances of mob-led witch burning or witch hanging in their tracks. Wherever the power of the Catholic Church was strong, witch crazes did not happen. Wherever the power of the Church was weak, they did. The people who led the witch hunts uniformly came from the most educated classes of society. They were people who refused to accept Church teaching, thinking they knew better themselves how to judge in these matters.

While Wiccans who are historians recognize the facts of the matter, Wiccans who read nothing but their own popular literature continue to promote the kinds of extraordinary inaccuracies which Mr. Brown puts in Robert Langdon's mouth.

For more information, see Jenny Gibson's marvelous article in issue # 5 of the *Pomegranate* or Professor Brian A. Pavlac's work, "Ten Common Errors and Myths about the Witch Hunts, Corrected and Commented."

SEX IS DIRTY
CHAPTER 28, PAGE 125

When a Jewish rabbi picks up the Torah to read it, he has to wash his hands immediately afterwards. Contact with the Torah "soils the hands." Why is this?

The answer is as simple as your own childhood experiences. When the streetlights went on at twilight, your mom called you home. When you approached the porch lights, what might she say? "Good heavens, dear, you are filthy! You need a bath!" Now, we had been outside playing all day long, and had never been conscience of our filth. It was only as we approached the light that we became aware of our need to wash.

The same is true with any holy thing. As we approach the holy, we become aware of our own imperfections, our own unwillingness to be what God intends us to be. Sex is holy. It is the pre-eminent way in which we can naturally participate in the life-giving richness who is God. Thus, as we approach the holiness of the sexual act, we become aware of the things within us that keep us from treating that enormous participation in divinity with the dignity and joy it deserves.

Many poorly catechized Christians have seen sex as dirty precisely because they understood what even the pagans understand – something special is going on here. Neither really understand what. They didn't have a well-catechized Catholic to teach them. Books like *Sex and the Sacred City* were, for the most part, not yet written (a great tragedy, if I do say so myself). Thus, many people continue to think the Catholic Church teaches that sex is dirty when, in fact, the Catholic Church teaches that sex is holy. In Langdon's universe it might be different, but calling sex dirty in our world is a complete perversion of Catholic teaching.

"WHAT KIND OF GOD WOULD WANT A BODY PUNISHED THIS WAY?"
CHAPTER 29, PAGE 128

Certainly not Christ. As has been pointed out, grace is God's presence in the world, grace is power. Because God has given us free will and because He respects our free will, He allows us to shut Him out of the universe we inhabit. Now, He knows that if we shut Him out, the universe will not continue to function as it should. We will suffer if we do this. God does not want us to choose actions that will result in our pain and suffering. Sadly, we often disagree with God on this point. We tend to choose to act in ways that bring enormous suffering into the world. Then we blame Him because we broke the world.

Once we remove grace from the world, once we remove Him from the world, suffering is inevitably the result. Now it's just a question of who: who is going to suffer? Christ took an enormous amount of suffering onto Himself in order to help us avoid it. But His cross is not the end of the story. It is the beginning.

God always calls us to participate in His divinity. That means we have the opportunity to act as He acts. So, now he gives us a choice. Do we want to act as He did? He doesn't need our help to rid the world of suffering, but He allows us mere mortals to act as God, if we choose. If we have His presence within us, if we are in a state of grace, and if we decide to use the grace, act as He did and accept the suffering we experience in the world, then He unites our sacrifice to His own. Our pain becomes His pain.

His suffering brought the grace needed to heal the world – now, so does ours. We are real participants in His divinity. Pain, a natural evil is baptized and used for good. It is transformed. But this transformation requires us to be in a state of grace, it requires

God's presence in our lives, it requires us to be innocent. God makes us innocent through His sacraments, then He allows us to help Him heal the world. This is God's way.

If we did things God's way instead of our way, life would be radically better for all concerned. But as long as we insist on being Frank Sinatra, singing "I Did It My Way," the world will continue to be a pretty messed-up place.

THE MADONNA OF THE ROCKS
CHAPTER 30, PAGE 133

In our universe, that painting is on wood, not canvas, so Sophie would have a hard time putting her knee through it, unless she were a karate expert. In the FACT section, Dan Brown says, "All descriptions of artwork, architecture, documents, and secret rituals in this novel are accurate." Now, technically speaking, this describes the medium on which the art resides, not the art itself, so he hasn't violated the statement here.

TWO VERSIONS OF THE MADONNA OF THE ROCKS
CHAPTER 32, PAGES 138-139

Leonardo did indeed paint two versions of the *Madonna of the Rocks*, with the original hung in the Louvre, and the second version in the Grand Gallery of London. The similarities between our world and Langdon's world begin and end there.

In Langdon's universe, the original Madonna of the Rocks hung in the Louvre shows John the Baptist blessing Christ, Mary with a claw-like extension of her hand and Uriel making a cutting gesture with his hand. Although it isn't clear what the similarities and differences are since Langdon doesn't describe the second painting at all, Langdon's alternate reality clearly has two versions of the paintings that are radically at odds with one another.

In our universe, however, the two paintings are virtually identical. In both, John the Baptist is shown with his hands folded in prayer, while Christ blesses him with the classic blessing hand: two-fingers raised, three fingers folded down. This arrangement of Christ's fingers is typical Catholic artwork; the two raised fingers symbolize the two natures of Christ (human and divine) revealed in Jesus while the three folded fingers represent the three Persons of the Godhead hidden within the one divine nature. Likewise, both paintings show the Madonna stretching a protective hand over her Child.

This protecting hand is reminiscent of the baldachino typically found over the altar in older Catholic churches. The canopy or baldachin represents the presence of divine power beneath. Up until very recent times, the Pope traveled under a portable baldachin because he is Christ's steward on earth.

The only major difference between the two paintings lies in the detail of how John's prophetic mission is visually represented. John the Baptist typically carries a staff topped with a cross. This is missing in the first painting and supplied in the second. Meanwhile, the angel Uriel is pointing at John the Baptist in the first painting, but is not pointing at him in the second.

Why would Uriel point at John the Baptist? Because Uriel is the angel of prophecy and John the Baptist is the greatest prophet, for he most fully prepared the way for the Messiah. In the first painting, Uriel's pointing finger emphasizes the fulfillment of Old Testament prophecy and John's prophetic mission: a perfectly reasonable Catholic theme.

However, by substituting the staff with cross for Uriel's pointing finger, John's role is transformed. Now John is still the prophet, but the presence of the Cross makes him the prophet of Christ's salvific suffering. That is, with this single change, the painting transforms from an emphasis on John as the prophet of the Messiah to John as the prophet of the suffering Messiah.

In a Catholic Church, the altar is the place of sacrifice, it is where Christ's single sacrifice is made present. Through the sacrifice of the Mass, Catholics join the Blessed Virgin Mary, the apostle John and Mary Magdalene, in a certain sense, and stand with them at the foot of the Cross. Since this painting was meant to be the centerpiece for an altar, the change is perfectly appropriate.

VATICAN II TEMPERED CHURCH LAW
CHAPTER 34, PAGE 149

Again, Langdon's universe stands in stark contrast to our own, but in this instance, it is hard to say exactly what happened in Langdon's alternate universe. The law of the Church is canon law. In our universe, Vatican II didn't say a single thing concerning canon law. Langdon never tells us what "Church law" was tempered in his alternate reality. Given the description, it is hard to believe that the Vatican II in Langdon's fabricated world tracked very closely with our own.

One might think that Mr. Brown meant Vatican II tempered Church doctrine. But it didn't. Vatican II teaches exactly the same doctrines the Church has always taught, as any serious reading of the documents quickly demonstrates. True, most modern commentators on Vatican II don't mention this. After all, most such commentators haven't bothered to actually sit down and read the documents. They just repeat rumors of rumors, each re-telling more wild than its predecessor.

Perhaps Langdon meant "law" in the sense of liturgical practice; "the law of prayer is the law of faith," as the old saying goes. While it is true that the liturgy underwent some modifications in the years following the council, most of these changes, such as having the priest face the people during Mass, the translation of the entire Mass into the vernacular, the movement of the tabernacle away from the center of the church, etc., were not mandated or even mentioned by the Council. Indeed, some of the changes, such as the sudden de-emphasis on Gregorian chant, were exactly the opposite of what the Council ordered. So even this sense of the phrase does not correspond to our universe. Vatican II did not order most of the liturgical changes erroneously attributed to it.

In this world, no matter how we try to interpret the words "Church law," we come up empty. None of it corresponds to what we know. Dan Brown's fictional version of the Second Vatican Council sounds quite interesting. It's a pity we never find out what sort of nuttiness his fake version of the Catholic Church indulged in. But, this is often the way things go in alternate universe novels.

PEOPLE DON'T NEED INDULGENCE

CHAPTER 34, PAGE 149

In a rather clever inside joke, Mr. Brown has the bishop of Opus Dei say that people don't need to be given comfort and indulgence. This is a subtle reference to the fact that the Catholic Church in our universe still teaches indulgences, just as Christians did from apostolic times forward. Indeed, Pope John Paul II instituted a whole new raft of them for the Jubilee year 2000.

Unfortunately, his fictional Catholic Church appears to have done away with them, since the heretical Opus Dei bishop is pleased at their disappearance. This is one of the clues that his is an alternate reality Opus Dei. Real Opus Dei members are well acquainted with the practice of indulgences and embrace them wholeheartedly. Similarly, the Church can never teach that indulgences don't exist. They do. Since the Church teaches only what is true, the teachings can never be "tempered" or "done away with."

BISHOP ARINGAROSA IS A FIDEIST
CHAPTER 34, PAGE 149

In another subtle illustration of just how crazy an alternate universe can get, Dan Brown has the Opus Dei bishop, the bishop of one of the most orthodox organizations in the Catholic Church, embrace the condemned heresy of fideism. Fideism is a philosophy or attitude that says unaided human reason cannot discover the truth. Reason is not the criterion of truth, authority is. A fideist will say, "I believe it only because the Church teaches it, the teaching does not need to be in accord with reason."

Since fideists insist faith is the only way to come to knowledge of God, they often oppose scientific inquiry. The logic of science and reason is insufficient and has essentially no place in religion. Now, every generation tends to re-invent their grandfathers' heresies, and they generally believe themselves to be quite original thinkers when they do. Fideism is no stranger to this practice. It was condemned in 1348, 1832, 1834 and 1855.

In our generation, Pope John Paul II repeated the exercise, recently writing an entire encyclical (*Faith and Reason*, 1998) showing why faith and reason are both critical to being a good Catholic. If either are missing, the Faith cannot be held or transmitted. Langdon's alternate universe appears thoroughly infected with this heresy, however, as both Opus Dei and Langdon espouse it. See "Faith is based on fabrication, acceptance of that which we imagine to be true, that which we cannot prove," Chapter 82, page 341.

THE KNIGHTS TEMPLAR
CHAPTER 38, PAGE 159

In Langdon's universe, the Pope stood behind the downfall of the Knights. In our universe, it was the French king Philip the Fair, grandson of St. Louis, who engineered the arrest of the Templars without the Pope's knowledge or consent. Once Pope Clement V discovered what had happened, he protested Philip's arrest and torture of the Knights, annulled the trials and suspended the powers of the bishops involved.

However, since seventy-two of the Templars stood before the skeptical Pope and admitted guilt, the Pope had to continue the trials. In an effort to exonerate them, he extended it to the whole Templar organization in all the countries of Europe. Most of these trials found the Templars innocent, but in France, the King controlled the process. The power of the French Templars was broken.

Incidentally, the Pope was not in the Vatican during this period. He lived in Avignon, which is one of the reasons he had rather more difficulty than usual stopping Philip. Needless to say, since none of the principles were in Rome, no one's ashes got scattered in the Tiber.

FRIDAY THE 13ᵀᴴ IS UNLUCKY
CHAPTER 38, PAGE 160

This day is considered a day of ill omen because Christ, the head of a group of 13 men, got crucified on Friday. This fact used to be pretty well-known in European culture, even meriting mention by one of the characters in the TV adaptation of Agatha Christie's popular novel "Lord Edgeware Dies." The movie was titled "Thirteen at Dinner."

"POP SCHLOCKMEISTER"
CHAPTER 38, PAGE 162

Robert Langdon's editor has to specifically refute the idea that Langdon is a "pop schlockmeister looking for a quick buck." If Langdon occupied our universe, we might quote Shakespeare in saying that Mr. Brown doth protest too much.

THE GRAIL LEGENDS ARE UNIQUE
CHAPTER 38, PAGE 164

Actually, the True Cross, the crown of thorns and the Shroud of Turin all inspired similar legendary searches. The major differences are these: (1) the other legendary searches eventually found their object, and (2) none of the searches happened in England, so they aren't part of American-English history as the Arthurian legend is.

NOAH WAS AN ALBINO
CHAPTER 39, PAGE 167

Mr. Brown provides another clue to the fact that his is an alternate universe. In his world, the Book of Enoch is apparently part of the Christian Bible, since this reference to Noah's albinism can only be found there (1 Enoch 106:2). In our world, NOAH is the National Organization for Albinism and Hypopigmentation. Thus, for readers, this assertion is nothing more than a fairly silly pun about NOAH and albinos made at the reader's expense.

However, it should be noted that in this pun, Mr. Brown also pokes fun at his own plot. At one point, he has Langdon say, "Misunderstanding breeds distrust" (page 45). This is, of course, precisely what Mr. Brown has done by making an albino one of the premier villains in the novel. As NOAH members point out, albinos are always typecast as villains. Thus, Langdon pontificates (pardon the pun) on how satanic goddess symbols are misunderstood. Yet, he is pursued by (a) an albino Catholic, (b) who insists on dressing as a monk (c) and whips himself. Each one of these things: albinism, Catholicism, monks (men wearing what look like dresses), and self-flagellation are sources of misunderstanding with the rest of the world.

Oddly, Langdon doesn't mention the nudity, the goddess initiation ritual of being spanked with a sharp sword or similarly misunderstood aspects of Wicca. The discerning reader will find Mr. Brown's inside joke here the height of hilarity.

HIDDEN MEANINGS WHERE NONE EXIST
CHAPTER 40, PAGE 171

In this sentiment, our universe and Langdon's coincide. As has been seen, if Langdon were not occupying an alternate universe, this charge would be laid at his door in spades. As it is, Mr. Brown answers possible readers' objections simply by asserting that he hasn't made this mistake, a perfectly reasonable response as long as Langdon lives in a fabricated universe, where the color of his sky is different than our own.

SECRETARIAT VATICANA
CHAPTER 41, PAGE 173

There is no such office. The Vatican Secretary, which is perhaps meant to be the parallel office in our universe, has no control over funds.

LEONARDO QUOTES
CHAPTER 55, PAGE 231

Needless to say, Leonardo's quotes given here were not made in reference to the Bible. See the commentary on Chapter 20, page 96, Leonardo and 'goddess worship'.

THE BIBLE WAS NOT FAXED FROM HEAVEN
CHAPTER 55, PAGE 231

The entire conversation with Teabing contains multiple arguments that further solidify the difference between Langdon's artificial world and the real world we inhabit. Teabing's first point is one every Catholic agrees on. The Bible was written by men, collated by men, and established by men.

Have you ever known a man so well that you could finish his sentences for him (and perhaps frequently did) and he could do the same for you? Though you may have had radically different upbringings, your understanding of the world and his understanding of the world on certain points was so close that you could virtually read each other's minds. That's how it was with the authors of the Scriptures and God. ·

The men who wrote the Bible wrote it through the divine inspiration of God Himself. The New Testament writers carried the apostolic authority of God, entrusted to them by Christ in John 21. They were nothing more than men, but their upbringing, their theological training, their way of looking at the world on certain points was so precisely God's way of looking at the world on those same points that they were able to write down exactly what they wanted to say, while at the same time writing exactly what God wanted to say, no more, no less. They finished God's sentences for Him. Yes, they were just men, but they were instruments. Yes they were instruments, but they were true authors of Scripture even though God was Scripture's true author.

So the Bible did not arrive by fax from heaven. It didn't have to. God is Truth. He describes how the world works so that we might live in it blissfully. There were men already here who understood how the world worked. They just wrote it down.

Since quill was first set to papyrus, men have always tried to change the contents of the Scriptures, whether they be the Sadducees, who rejected everything but the first five books of the Old Testament, or men like Luther, who rejected several more books of the Old Testament and nearly rejected a half-dozen New Testament books like Hebrews and James to boot. This is not news. Still, we have more copies of Scripture than all other ancient writings combined. Given the enormous numbers of languages and the vast breadth of geography over which these texts have been discovered, the miracle lies precisely in the fact that the various versions match so closely. Indeed, no other ancient document can lay this claim, or even come close to laying this claim.

MORE THAN EIGHTY GOSPELS WERE CONSIDERED
CHAPTER 55, PAGE 231

In Langdon's universe, created by the hand of Mr. Brown, this is undoubtedly true. After all, Mr. Brown has the freedom to create whatever alternate reality he wishes.

In our universe, however, the number of Gospels was fixed at four well before the turn of the first century. In fact, according to some scholars, the entire New Testament, with the possible exception of the book of Revelation, was already written by the destruction of Jerusalem in 70 A.D. The last book, the book of Revelation, was completed by the year 100 A.D.

Even the first-century Ebionite heretics embraced the Gospel of Matthew. Independent witnesses such as Tertullian and Justin Martyr (150 A.D.), and Iraeneus (170 A.D.) attest to Matthew, Mark, Luke and John being the only four Gospels in existence. Indeed, these four Gospels are so extensively quoted in the writings of the early Christians that we could virtually reconstruct all four from those sources alone. The Gnostic Gospels are barely mentioned in comparison.

Meanwhile, none of the pivotal writings referred to in these chapters of Mr. Brown's fiction would even be written until at least 150 A.D., and most would not appear for a century after that. Unlike the four Gospels, which were all known to have been written by the people to whom they are attributed, the Gnostic Gospels, such as the Gospels of Peter, Philip, Mary Magdalene and others, were written well after their namesakes were already in the grave. So, Mr. Brown does not violate his first promise here either. These documents do exist, he just doesn't bother to mention that none of them were written as fiction, or that they were often written hundreds of years after the plot in his novel already required their presence.

Some excellent books that discuss the compilation of the Bible are: *Redating the New Testament* by John Robinson or *The New Testament Documents: Are They Reliable?* by F.F. Bruce, *Lost Christianities: The Battles for Scriptures and the Faiths We Never Knew,* by Dr. Bart Ehrman, *The Nag Hammadi Library,* edited by James M. Robinson. For a quick overview of how the Bible came to be, see the chapter on Scripture in *Bible Basics* by Steve Kellmeyer.

THE BIBLE WAS COLLATED BY CONSTANTINE

CHAPTER 55, PAGE 231

Constantine had nothing to do with the collation of the Bible. The first formally approved list of both the Old and the New Testaments was given by Pope Damasus in 382. It was confirmed at the Councils of Hippo and Carthage in 393 and 397 respectively. Incidentally, this list of books includes books that

Brown and others would rather omit: Tobias, Judith, Wisdom, Ecclesiasticus, Baruch, 1 and 2 Maccabees, parts of Esther (chapters 10-16, or A-F), and parts of Daniel (3:24-90 and 13, 14). Constantine had been in his grave for over a half century when the list of Bibleical books was formally assembled.

CONSTANTINE WAS BAPTIZED AGAINST HIS WILL
CHAPTER 55, PAGE 232

There is no evidence this charge is true. He did wait until near the end of his life to be baptized, but that was not unusual in his time. Baptism washes away not only sin, but the temporal punishment for sin. Thus, anyone who is baptized immediately prior to his death does not need a long public penance for post-baptismal sins, nor does he need to be purified in Purgatory before entering heaven. In the early Church, many converts to the Faith put off baptism, gambling that they could get baptized and completely cleansed immediately before death.

ROME'S OFFICIAL RELIGION WAS SUN-WORSHIP
CHAPTER 55, PAGE 232

Rome's official religion was the worship of Jupiter, Juno, Minerva, etc. Constantine and his father were members of the Sol Invictus sun worship cult, but that didn't make it Rome's official religion. While Christianity had indeed grown explosively, it had made inroads only among slaves and the lower classes. Virtually none of the officials of Rome were Christian, nor were many of the soldiers or their leaders. Constantine had no burning political reason to embrace Christianity. But Constantine had experienced an enormous military victory in the sign of the Cross, and he believed.

The Edict of Milan did not make Christianity the official religion, nor would it become Rome's official religion under Constantine. It would take another fifty years after his death before that happened. The Edict simply made Christianity a legal religion. That meant Christians could no longer be fed to lions or covered with tar and burned alive. Romans were still free to ignore Christianity, and Roman leaders often continued to do just that.

ISIS NURSING INSPIRED ICONS OF MARY NURSING
CHAPTER 55, PAGE 232

In Langdon's universe, if the Egyptians had not portrayed Isis nursing Horus, it would never have occurred to anyone to show Mary's maternal love by painting her nursing Jesus.

The idea is so silly, it could only come from a man. I've never seen an icon of Isis nursing Horus, and I doubt you have either. Still, we have both seen nursing mothers, and we recognize the sign of love between them the moment we see the way a child suckling at his mother's breast looks up at his mother, and the way she looks down at him.

It seems highly unlikely that even the people in Langdon's alternate universe really needed to see Isis and Horus to understand what happens in that moment between a mother and a child. The love between mother and child is an eternal truth, and artists everywhere have throughout eternity tried to capture it. As long as they continue to try, there is hope for us.

NOTHING IN CHRISTIANITY IS ORIGINAL

CHAPTER 55, PAGE 232

While this is certainly true of Gardner's invention of Wicca, it is certainly not true of Christianity. No pagan literature bears any resemblance to the prophecies of the Old Testament or its constant divine insistence that people choose between the God of the Jews and everything else.

Similarly, there is nothing in any pagan religion that comes anywhere near the power and profundity of Christ's teaching and miracles. Unlike pagan myths, the historical accounts of Jesus' ministry, His life, death and resurrection, are tightly fixed into a specific geographic and historical context, with numerous non Christian sources corroborating the historical accuracy of the four Gospel accounts. Archeological digs continue to verify the historical accuracy of element after element of the Gospels in particular and the Scripture accounts in general. Nothing approaching this level of accuracy can be said about any pagan mythological tradition. The Christian tradition is not myth, it is historical fact.

Now, do some pagan symbols echo the truths expressed in Scripture? Sure. As was pointed out in the Chapter 1, page 7 discussion of pagan symbols in Chartres, if God took on human flesh and walked the earth to die and rise among us, it would be darned odd to discover that the echoes of this incredible event did not affect every culture that ever existed. Time is as much a created thing as the ground we walk on. Like a stone thrown into a pond, the effects of the Incarnation and Crucifixion ripple forward and backward through time and will necessarily find some expression in even the most pagan cultures.

CONSTANTINE SHIFTED THE SABBATH TO SUNDAY
CHAPTER 55, PAGE 232-233

Actually, the apostles did this, and they did it before Constantine's father was born. The fact can be easily verified. The New Testament shows that the apostles said that the Sabbath was not binding on Christians (Acts 15:1-29; Colossians 2:16-17), and that the early Church worshipped on the first day of the week to commemorate the Saviour's resurrection (Acts 20:7, 1 Corinthians 16:2). Numerous histories of the Church written before Constantine's rise to power confirm this, including the aforementioned Justin Martyr's work.

COUNCIL OF NICAEA VOTED ON JESUS' DIVINITY
CHAPTER 55, PAGE 233

Not exactly. Everyone at Nicaea agreed Christ is God. They also knew He is man. They met in order to decide how this whole divinity thing worked. Was Christ akin to an enormously powerful angel, acting as God to every created person including the angels as Bishop Arius said or did He actually possess the one divine nature totally to Himself as virtually everyone but Bishop Arius said?

The bishops meeting in council compared notes on what the apostles had taught them and their successors, and they all agreed: Christ totally possessed the one divine nature. The vote wasn't even close – 313 to five, which quickly became 316 to 2 when three of the bishops changed their votes. The council fathers also decided the date for Easter.

The bishops burned Arius' writings, but nothing else. Constantine exiled Arius, but later recalled him. True, Constantine had called the council in order to bring peace to his empire after the long dispute between Arius and the rest of Christendom, but he avoided the council chambers and the debates except for the opening welcome and the closing farewell.

The idea that the early Church totally destroyed all material that contradicted Catholic Faith is not new to Dan Brown's novel. It has been promoted for years among certain fundamentalist Christians in order to solve a vexing theological problem.

Most Christian denominations believe themselves to be following the lifestyle and devotional practices recommended by Scripture and taught by the apostles. However, when they compare their own practices to those in the earliest available historical Christian documents, they invariably discover that their practices do not, in fact, conform to the practices of those earliest Christians, the men and women who had been taught by the apostles.

Their replies to this fact have been two-fold. First, the historical sources are repudiated as being non-Scriptural and therefore prone to error. Second, nefarious Catholics, generally led by Constantine, are accused of having hounded the true Christians into historical obscurity and having burned all of the true historical accounts of correct Christian worship and practice. They point to the lack of any historical evidence for their beliefs as evidence of how thorough the Catholic Church's destructive methods were.

The problem, of course, is precisely that practice of Catholic Faith was legalized barely twenty years prior to Constantine's death. Prior to that, Catholics were a persecuted minority, often living in fear of their lives. How did this minority of the population whose popularity lay mainly among the lower classes get the political clout to totally destroy all evidence of opposition throughout the entire Roman Empire in such a short time? The answer is simple: it didn't. That kind of organization and power has never been possessed even by 20ᵗʰ century totalitarian regimes with the latest technology, much less the kind of steel sword and wooden wheel culture the Romans lived in. Even pagan historians leave us no record of the kind of activity that would have been necessary for such mass historical erasures.

But the myth persists. All Mr. Brown has done is change the content of the mythical documents. With fundamentalist Christians, the contents of these non-existent documents described their fundamentalist belief system to a "T." With the characters in this novel, the contents of the non-existent documents prove that Jesus was not God, He was just a normal guy like the rest of us. There's the irony: a myth originally developed to justify the existence of man-made Christian denominational practice is now being used to justify goddess worship. Christians have no one to blame but themselves.

An excellent book summarizing the events of Niceae, the first Council of the Church, is Philip Hughes' *The Church in Crisis: A History of the General Councils*. Dozens of other scholarly books have been written, and none of them say what Teabing says.

CONSTANTINE AND THE VATICAN POWER BASE
CHAPTER 55, PAGE 233

During Constantine's time, Vatican Hill was a deserted graveyard. Now, archaeology shows that a Christian shrine at St. Peter's grave has existed since the time of Pope Anicetus, circa 150 A.D., and was a destination for Christian pilgrims in the 200 and 300's A.D. It seems that the tilework in front of Peter's grave had to be replaced in the 200's due to the enormous numbers of pilgrims. Their knees wore out the stones.

CONSTANTINE COMMISSIONED A NEW BIBLE
CHAPTER 55, PAGE 234

He did no such thing. Indeed, he permitted pagan worship to continue up to his own death. The Bible commissioning is most assuredly an "alternate universe" historical point, since there is no evidence anywhere of any such thing happening.

LEONARDO'S *LAST SUPPER*
CHAPTER 55, PAGE 235-250

In Langdon's world, the *Last Supper* is a fresco portraying the moment of consecration, when Christ pronounces the words "This is my body... This is my blood... " and Mary Magdalene is seated next to Jesus. All of his interpretation hinges on these two "alternate world" changes to the painting.

Let's deal with the last objection first. Langdon's world is completely uncontaminated by Leonardo's own *Treatise on Painting* in which the artist tells us exactly what he was doing. He firmly believed in presenting visual "types." When an artist paints according to "type" the viewer is given all the visual clues necessary to determine the class of person being viewed. The person's age and station is made clearly known. Old men will therefore be portrayed in one way, mature men who carry the fullness of power in another way, young men who have not yet reached maturity are represented in a third way, and boys in a fourth. But not just age will be made apparent. The kind of work they do, their level of wisdom, all of this will also influence the visual presentation. This mode of visual presentation was extremely common in the Renaissance, and Leonardo believed it to be an excellent way of going about his work.

Of the several dozen "types" available for visual presentation, the "student" was certainly prominent. Such men are always shown with long hair and without beard, for they have not yet reached the age where a man can grow a decent beard. The student is young, inexperienced, hanging on the Master's every word trying to understand the world.

St. John, being the youngest of the apostles and "the disciple Jesus loved," was always portrayed in this fashion. For instance, look at any painting or statuary in which he is depicted at the foot of the Cross – a location in which Mary Magdalene and Mary, the Mother of God, will also be found – and the similarities to Leonardo's depiction will become immediately obvious. Leonardo didn't depict Mary Magdalene. He depicted St. John. That's why ABC News had to interview a dozen different art historians before they found anyone who was willing to agree with Langdon's thesis. To be quite blunt, art historians know this is silly. ABC News discovered it was hard to find anyone willing to trade fame in the public sphere for ridicule within their own profession.

The people within the painting are arranged in groups of three because the artist captured the moment of betrayal, as the disciples all disclaimed the idea that they would ever betray Jesus, a theme common to Italian depictions of the Last Supper. By placing all the disciples on the same side of the table, we can see how the effects of this statement ripple out through the groups. Judas, Peter and John are grouped because they show the three reactions to Jesus: Judas betrays and does not return, Peter abandons Him but does return, John alone neither betrays nor abandons Christ.

This also explains why everyone still has their own cup. The Passover meal has four ritual cups of wine associated with it. The third cup, called the cup of blessing, is the one Jesus consecrates. Immediately after the consecration, He and the disciples leave the meal, for Christ intends to drink the fourth cup, the cup of consummation, while hanging on the Cross. But the announcement of the betrayal does not happen at the consecration of the cup of blessing. In fact, the Gospel of John upon which the painting is based does not describe the Last Supper consecrations at all. That's why Leonardo's painting is called *The Last Supper*, not *The Eucharist* or *The Third Cup*.

Likewise, the word "chalice" comes from the Greek word "kalyx" or "cup." The word refers to the hollow part of anything. While 21st century Americans tend to think of a chalice as a particular kind of cup with a stem, the Greeks had no such preconceptions. The presence or absence of cups versus chalices is not relevant.

Finally, the painting is tempera on stone, not fresco.

For further information on this painting, read the work of decent art historians such as Elizabeth Lev, who teaches at Duquesne University's Rome campus. See also the commentary on chapter 58, page 248 for an explanation of the dagger in the painting.

"HERETIC" WAS FIRST USED BY CONSTANTINE

CHAPTER 55, PAGE 234

The term "heretic" comes from the Greek word "airesis." The word "airesis" is used by Josephus to describe the Sadducees, the Pharisees and the Essenes. Josephus wrote well before his death in 100 A.D., that is, he used it in this sense about 200 years before Constantine and the Council of Nicaea. St. Paul is called an *aireseos*, or leader of the Nazarene heresy in Acts 24:5, when he is turned over to the Roman governor Felix. The Jews in Rome say the same about Christians in Acts 28:22. All Scripture scholars agree that Acts was written prior to 100 A.D. St. Justin uses *airesis* in the same sense in his Dialogue with Trypho, chapter 18, verse 108 around 150 A.D. and St. Peter uses it to describe false Christian sects in 2

Peter 2:1. Before Constantine's father was even a gleam in his grandfather's eye, the Church was already condemning anyone who chose not to accept the authority of bishops, the divinely authorized teachers, as a heretic.

THE CHALICE, THE BLADE, AND HIEROS GAMOS
CHAPTER 56, PAGES 237-239

This entire section is imported from the Wicca religion that Gardner invented in 1939. It is quite a commentary on Gerald Gardner that he used a blade as a phallic symbol when he created the Wicca religion. It is an equally strong comment on Wicca that this symbolism is retained to this very day. After all, how many women really enjoy the image of a sharp knife slicing in between their legs? Yet, if the "blade" is meant to represent a penis, as Teabing and Langdon assert, isn't that exactly the image these nature-worshipping men symbolically intend to reproduce in their Hieros Gamos: a sharp blade slicing up through a woman's vagina and in towards her womb?

This explains something else. It is often noted that a significant number of the staff in a certain kind of medical clinic adhere to Wicca. The reason for this is now much more clear. What happens in ritual Wiccan ceremony is exactly what happens during the surgical procedure many Wiccans actively champion: abortion.

"Goddess-friendly" religions tend to be misogynistic in their symbols, rituals and outlooks, and Wicca is no exception to the rule. See *"La lingua pura,"* Chapter 72, page 303, "Jesus' marriage," Chapter 58, pages 244-245 and "Quoting the Gospel of Mary Magdalene," Chapter 58, page 24.

CHRISTIANITY: MAN-CREATOR, WOMAN-SINNER
CHAPTER 56, PAGE 238

In God, there is neither male nor female. God is not a man anymore than God is a woman. God is neither. He is referred to with a male pronoun because God is always the first actor – He penetrates us with His grace, we don't penetrate Him. He gives life, we receive life. He acts, we react. The closest analogy we have for this in our own experience is the life-giving act of sex, in which man acts, he penetrates woman, woman reacts, she has a child nine months later.

As for Christian Scripture laying the burden on Eve, there are two replies. First, Genesis is originally Jewish Scripture. It was written at least three millenia prior to the birth of Jesus. Second, while New Testament Scriptures assert twice that Eve was deceived (2 Cor 11:3 and 1 Tit 2:13), those same Scriptures blame Adam exclusively for both the trespass itself and for being the cause of death (Rom 5:14 and 1 Cor 15:22). Eve was tricked, but Adam was responsible. He was supposed to have protected her from the serpent. Eve may have eaten of the fruit, but only after Adam ate of it were "the eyes of both of them opened." His collusion caused the Fall and its consequences.

Indeed, it was precisely Adam's fault that required God's incarnation. Adam was the first and therefore the most powerful patriarch; he had responsibility for and authority over creation. When he refused God's grace, only a man who had more authority than Adam could reverse the decision and welcome God's grace back into the world. That's why God became man. Only by taking on human nature and becoming man Himself could God both show His respect for Adam's authority and also heal the problems Adam's decision had caused. The Son of God, through whom Adam was created, became the only man with more authority than Adam.

MARY MAGDALENE'S SMEAR CAMPAIGN
CHAPTER 58, PAGE 244

The Church declared Mary Magdalene a saint and went to rather serious lengths to preserve her relics. While it is true that Scripture says Mary Magdalene had seven demons driven from her (Mark 16:9), it also points out that she was one of those who ministered to Christ (Luke 8:2-3). All four Gospel accounts put her at the foot of the Cross. All four indicate that she was one of the women who went to tend to His body after the Sabbath, and all four explicitly name her as the first witness of the Resurrection. The Church has always named her "apostle to the apostles." If this is a smear campaign, it's very poorly done.

The question about her possible association with prostitution comes from the fact that Christ was anointed either once or twice before His death. Three different Gospels attest to an anointing prior to the Crucifixion; opinions differ on whether these were two separate anointings or just a single anointing related by three different Gospel authors (Matthew 26:1;3, Mark 14:3-9, John 12:1-8). In any case, the descriptions agree that the anointing was done by a woman or women of less than savoury reputation.

Since the woman or women who did this anointing is (are) not named, there have long been disputes about who she/they might be. This is made more difficult by the fact that Matthew, Mark and Luke were written while many of the people named within the Gospels were still alive. Unlike the gossip columnists of today, the Gospel writers had a habit of not revealing the names of living people who might be seen in a bad light; thus Luke says the tax collector is named Levi, and refrains from pointing out that Levi has another name: Matthew. Certainly prostitution was viewed no more favorably than tax collection, and the first three Gospels, at least, would have good reason to draw a veil over the identity of the woman in question.

Since John's Gospel was written decades after the other three, however, he had no reason to veil identities; the principles involved were dead. He identifies Mary of Bethany as the one who anointed Jesus' feet and he makes explicit Jesus' words of blessing over her. Now, he prominently places Mary Magdalene at the foot of the Cross. Were Mary of Bethany and Mary Magdalene the same person? Quite possibly.

The Greek Christians, the ones converted by Paul, agree that Mary Magdalene lived and died with the apostle John and Mary, Mother of God, in Ephesus. French tradition holds that she and some disciples went to Provence, France, where they converted the region, but that tradition is very late tenth century. If Mary Magdalene is indeed from the tribe of Benjamin, then the Greek Christian tradition is probably correct. See the commentary on "The Royal Tribe of Benjamin," Chapter 58, page 248.

JESUS' MARRIAGE
CHAPTER 58, PAGES 244-245

Teabing is correct to argue that since Jewish law and custom essentially required a man to be married, Jesus must have been married. Jesus is, of course, married and has been for quite some time, as most Christians know.

The Old Testament prophesied the Messiah's marriage in the Song of Songs and Isaiah 62:5. Further, John the Baptist describes Jesus' marital status in John 3:28-30. John, however, makes the point Teabing misses. Jesus is the Bridegroom, but he is not married to a single woman, He is married to the Church. Every baptized person who joins himself or herself to the divine Spouse, the Church, becomes part of that divine marriage.

Paul confirms this marriage between God and man in Ephesians 5:21-33, among other places, and the Catholic Church has taught Christians about Jesus' marriage for two millenia. Indeed, the requirement for Jewish men to marry was divinely intended to train us into understanding that the source of our salvation is the sacrament of marriage itself.

God marries Himself to us through the sacrament of baptism. It is matured through the grace of the sacrament of confirmation. The marriage is consummated when the flesh of the Bridegroom enters the flesh of the Bride at the Nuptial Feast, the Mass. Eucharist is the Body, Blood, Soul and Divinity of Jesus Christ. He enters the Bride, His Church, and gives us life, just as He promised He would in John 6. *Sex and the Sacred City,* the book on the theology of the body, shows quite clearly how the sacraments marry us into the inner life of the Trinity. This is the Hieros Gamos that Egyptian pagans dimly sought but failed to grasp. See "The Chalice, the Blade, and Hieros Gamos," Chapter 56, pages 237-239.

"COMPANION" MEANS "WIFE" IN ARAMAIC

CHAPTER 58, PAGE 246

Fascinating, but irrelevant. Teabing says this in reference to the Gospel of Philip. Unfortunately, the only surviving copy of the Gospel of Philip is in Coptic, the language which served as an intermediary tool to get the Greek Gospels translated for the Egyptian. The Coptic text is therefore almost certainly a translation from an original Greek manuscript. There is no evidence the manuscript ever existed in Aramaic.

Jesus spoke three languages: Greek, Aramaic and Hebrew. Philip would likewise speak at least those three languages. While the Gospels of Matthew, Luke and John carry traces of Aramaic speech and grammar, Philip is not so blessed. It was also composed much later than the first four Gospels, that is, it was composed at a time when Greek Gentiles dominated the Church. Scholars agree that it was not composed until the late second or possibly early third century. Thus, there is no evidence the apostle Philip wrote it, and even if he did write it, there is no evidence he wrote it in anything except Greek.

But it gets worse. The Gospel of Philip is from the school of Valentinus (who died around 160), a Gnostic missionary in Egypt who wanted to be the bishop of Rome. Now, why on earth would an Egyptian want to be bishop of Rome in 150 A.D., given the enormous persecution the Church there routinely experienced, unless Rome had some kind of special prominence in Church authority? Now we see the real problem: the Gospel of Philip is not evidence of a marriage between Jesus and Mary Magdalene. If anything, the historical context of the Gospel of Philip is a demonstration of the authority of the bishop of Rome. Teabing is clearly misleading Sophia, but the plot never goes on to explain why.

QUOTING THE GOSPEL OF MARY MAGDALENE
CHAPTER 58, PAGE 247

Langdon is rather selective in his quotes. He completely omits the last verse of the *Gospel of Thomas*: "Simon Peter said to them, 'Make Mary leave us, for females don't deserve life.' Jesus said, 'Look, I will guide her to make her male, so that she too may become a living spirit resembling you males. For every female who makes herself male will enter the kingdom of Heaven.'" (*Gospel of Thomas*, verse 114). He also manages to leave out the verses immediately preceding the *Gospel of Mary Magdalene* quote: "Then Mary stood up and greeted all of them and said to her brethren, 'Do not mourn or grieve or be irresolute, for his grace will be with you all and will defend you. Let us rather praise his greatness, for he prepared us and made us into men.' When Mary said this, their hearts changed for the better, and they began to discuss the words of the [Savior]." (*Gospel of Mary Magdalene*, chapter 5, verses 2-4).

Again, both of these Gnostic works were written in the late third century, long after all the witnesses to Christ's life were dead. The Gnostic Gospels are not Scripture: they agreed that women could not enter heaven unless they became like men. That's why Christians rejected them. It was an absurd heresy to say that women could not enter heaven or had less of a chance to enter heaven than men did. But it was very much in accord with goddess religion. See "The Chalice, the Blade, and Hieros Gamos," Chapter 56, pages 237-239, and "Jesus instructs Mary Magdalene," Chapter 58, page 248.

PETER'S AUTHORITY

CHAPTER 58, PAGES 247-248

Unfortunately, Teabing fails to be consistent in his argument. On pages 244-245, he argues that Jesus was an orthodox Jew bound by custom, but now on page 248, he argues that Jesus was a radical who didn't care about custom. Which one is it? In fact, Jesus couldn't have left the governance of the Church to a woman precisely because that would violated the divine order that Jewish faith embodied.

It is anathema for orthodox Jewish women to have spiritual authority over men. Orthodox Jewish women can't be in the same room in prayer with orthodox Jewish men – they have to be in a separate room with an opaque screen erected to keep the sexes apart. Orthodox Jewish women cannot even study with Orthodox men. Remember *Yentl*, the Barbara Streisand movie that won Golden Globes for best picture and best director in 1983? Streisand played a woman who disguises herself as a man in order to get into yeshiva to get an education. Even after two millenia, some Jewish customs don't change.

Serious Jews still maintain this custom, but Christians do not. Why the difference? Because every Jewish custom pointed towards some aspect of God's self-revelation in Christ. Christ came to show us what the fullness of each custom really pointed towards. Jews esteemed the Sabbath and rightly so, but they esteemed it for the wrong reason: the Sabbath was made for man, not man for the Sabbath.

Jews separated men from women in the study of divine things and in prayer, because this was a sign of the separation between God and man prior to the Incarnation. Once God takes on human flesh, however, the need for a sign pointing to the division between God and man disappears.

The Jews forbad women governance over men in spiritual matters in order to mirror the relationship between God and man. Both man and woman image God. Woman images God through her ability to conceive and nurture new life, man images God through his service to woman, including the service of proclaiming God's life of grace. God penetrates man with grace, man responds with the welling forth of new life within himself. In sex, man penetrates woman and woman responds with the welling forth of new life within herself. This is why Christ is Bridegroom and we are Bride.

JESUS INSTRUCTS MARY MAGDALENE
CHAPTER 58, PAGE 248

Teabing asserts that Jesus gave Mary Magdalene instructions on running the Church in the "unaltered" Gospel of Mary Magdalene. Not exactly. Examine the text at http://www.gnosis.org/library/marygosp.htm for yourself. Mary reports that she saw Jesus in a vision and then gives an account of what He purportedly says. The message she relates is such an esoteric mish-mash that the apostles can't make heads or tails out of it.

And how does Teabing know the Gospel of Mary Magdalene is unaltered? Only three fragments have ever been discovered and none of them are complete. In stark contrast some 5000 complete copies of the four standard Gospels exist in a variety of languages. See "Quoting the Gospel of Mary Magdalene," Chapter 58, page 247.

THE DAGGER IN *THE LAST SUPPER*
CHAPTER 58, PAGE 248

A close examination of the painting will show a knife at Judas' back. This is hardly surprising: Judas betrayed Christ. He was the backstabber. Leonardo neatly portrays him as such by showing how traitors generally meet their end – with their own knife stuck between their own ribs. Judas would in turn be betrayed by the priests at the Temple, who would allow him to suicide rather than back out of the deal he had made.

Indeed, the Gospel of Matthew provides a very interesting correlation between the way the priests treat Judas and the way Pilate treats Jesus. Both Judas and Pilate are about to be involved in the shedding of innocent blood, both attempt to get out of it: Judas throws the money back, Pilate washes his hands. Then the priests repudiate Judas in words remarkably similar to the words Pilate uses to repudiate the crowd: "See to it yourself!" The difference? The priests reject Judas' blood money, the crowd accepts the cleansing blood of Christ.

Both Leonardo's early sketches of the scene and the final restored work itself show that the hand and arm wielding the dagger belong to Peter, who will draw a sword in the Garden of Gethsemane and chop off a man's ear (John 18:10).

THE ROYAL TRIBE OF BENJAMIN
CHAPTER 58, PAGE 248

The tribe of Benjamin had royal blood only in the sense that the first king of Israel, Saul, was a member of that tribe. However, that royal inheritance was broken with the death of Saul and his sons in battle. The royal kingship passed to the house of David. With David's ascendancy, the house of Judah became the source of royal blood; no son of Benjamin ever ruled Israel again. Still, the apostle Paul gloried in being a member of this tribe (Rom 11:1, Phil 3:5); it was one of only two tribes – the other being the house of Judah – that stayed true to God's covenant.

Thus, even if Mary Magdalene's bloodline could be traced back to the house of Benjamin – a doubtful proposition – it would not mean she was of royal blood, since she would still have to be proven to be a descendant of Saul. Furthermore, given that Paul was not exactly known as a man who avoided controversy, why would he permit one of his kin to be unfairly overlooked? Wouldn't one of his many letters at least point out Mary's poor treatment?

Paul is the man who did not hesitate to point out that he had stood against Peter and chastised him to his face when Peter simply failed to share table with Gentile Christians (Gal 2:11). He is certainly not going to stand by and watch his own kinswoman be denied the headship of the Church if Jesus had truly given it to her, nor would he permit his kinswoman to be abused if she were the wife of Jesus! After all, Paul gave up everything in order to follow this man. He would be imprisoned, beaten and ultimately executed for love of Jesus. Peter would never have gotten away with such a powerplay. Only someone completely unacquainted with the Pauline letters would suggest such a thing.

THE "Q" DOCUMENT
CHAPTER 60, PAGE 256

Another inside joke by Dan Brown. In order to see why, you have to know something about the origins of the "Q" document theory. Germany did not become a nation until 1871, as a result of the Franco-Prussian war. Prior to that, it was divided up into a bunch of principalities and kingdoms of various sizes, one of the largest being Prussia. Bismarck wanted to unify German sentiment.

To do this, he instituted something called the "Kulturkampf" - the "culture war" in which the government worked hard to break the power of the Catholic Church. Catholic Faith was seen as an obstacle to German union since the Bavarian south was almost exclusively Catholic and looked more to Rome than it did to Berlin and the Protestant North. Bavarian allegiance had to be turned to the north, as did the allegiance of all German Catholics. Thus, Bismarck's attitude encouraged shoddy scholarship that defamed the Catholic Church in order to re-orient Catholics towards Berlin.

The supporters of Bismarck's culture war chose their line of attack carefully. They built a significant part of it around the question of the Catholic Church's infallible teaching that Matthew was the first Gospel. In order to do this, they had to propose a different Gospel as the first Gospel: they chose the Gospel of Mark.

To support this choice, they came up with what one theological wag calls "The Reader's Digest Condensed Gospel Theory of Scripture." The German professors arbitrarily decided that shorter literary works always precede longer works. Since Mark is the shortest Gospel, that would mean it was written first. Of course, according to this theory, the Reader's Digest Condensed Version of *Gone With the Wind* was written before Margaret Mitchell's novel, but Bible scholars don't read popular magazines, so the joke is lost on them. They faced a more serious problem than the scoffing jeers of the unwashed masses. German theologians had to explain where the "extra" material in Matthew came from. It couldn't come from Matthew because then they would have to admit that Matthew's Gospel was first. It had to have come from somewhere else? Where?

They solved this puzzle through an equally marvelous invention. Since three of the four Gospels seemed to tell a common story, they must all three be derived from a single common source: Quelle! We can see a sample of the immense intellectual wit these gentlemen possessed when we realize that "Quelle" is simply a German word that means "source." The name was quickly shortened to "Q," presumably in order to impress women at cocktail parties with professional theological banter.

The story they invented to accompany "Q" was pure genius. "Quelle" was the oral tradition passed down within the early Christian communities. As the Christian communities grew and separated into their specific geographical regions over time, the oral traditions within the separate communities would naturally diverge a bit from the original common oral tradition. This divergence would be additive - people would naturally add stories about Christ, each community adding slightly different stories to accomodate the needs of their region.

If this sounds a little like evolutionary theory applied to literature, it is. Darwinian theory was all the vogue in Europe at this time. Darwin's *Origin of Species* was first published in 1854. His *Descent of Man*, published in 1871, reinforced the concepts of the first book. The whole of Europe was alive with theories of race: the French spoke of a "French race", the Germans of a "German race", the English of an "English race". The 1871 Franco-Prussian war was seen by Europeans as a necessary step in man's evolution, since it involved a contest of primacy between the German and French races. Likewise, Alfred Dreyfus, a French Jew (ironically, he was born in 1854 along with *Origin of Species*) would be among the first to discover that the "Jewish race" was not welcome in post-Darwinian Europe. He would be put to a sham trial by the French on charges of espionage. Evolutionary theory was being used to explain everything.

Now, as we all know, evolutionary theory requires time to work. According to the "Q" theory, the Gospels we have today were all written hundreds of years after the Crucifixion. This would give enough time for the oral traditions to evolve into their own distinct forms. The differences in the three Gospel stories were attributed to the addition of fabricated quotes and stories from the various Christian communities, who each apparently said, "Well, Christ *would* have said or done something like this, so we'll just put the words in His mouth and pretend He did." The oral "Q" source was said to form the common basis for the Gospels of Matthew, Mark and Luke, the differences came from the various communities.

Now, notice the problem Langdon has created for himself. If the "Q" theory is true, and if Constantine *did* commission a new Bible, he wouldn't have any of the Gospels of Matthew, Mark, Luke or John to put in it. After all, they were all still being written by the various faith communities in various far-off geographical regions at the same time Constantine is assembling his Bible. Remember, for the "Q" theory to work, a long period of time has to pass, and there has to be real trouble communicating between the various communities so that the different versions can evolve properly. Of course, if this were really the case, it means Constantine can't communicate with these faith communities very well either: he can't get the Gospels he needs. Indeed, he doesn't even know they exist. Furthermore, if "Q" is an *oral* tradition (which it has to be in order for the additions to be made without anyone noticing), then there can't be a "Q" document.

Now, one could assume, as Langdon and Teabing do, that Jesus wrote this "Q" document in His own hand. But it isn't wise: the German theologians were smart enough to specify an oral tradition for a reason. Sure, having a "Q" document solves the long "lapse of time" problem of "evolutionary" oral tradition, but it creates a much worse problem. There aren't any copies of "Q" anywhere, or even any references to "Q" anywhere. No one pretends to have seen a Gospel according to Jesus. For all the other ancient documents we know about, we either have a copy of some fragment of that document, or we have a mention of the document in another document. For "Q" – a document whose existence is purely a 19th-century academic theory – we have nothing at all. No other documents describe such a thing, no fragments of it have been found. And the very suggestion that it was a written document violates the original evolutionary theory, which requires that "Q" has to be an oral tradition for several centuries at least. You see, if it is a written document, then it *can't form the basis for Matthew, Mark or Luke.*Somebody would have noticed the additions because it would be possible to compare documents. If "Q" is oral, we can explain the lack of confirming documents; if it is written, the whole thing falls apart through lack of evidence.

Thus, the phrase "Q document" is as much a contradiction in terms as the phrase "holy sin" or "square circle". By asserting that the Sangreal treasure contains documents like the "Q document... written in Christ's own hand," Brown is quietly providing us with an amusing joke, a notice to an alert, well-informed reader that his entire novel is just a set of silly puns and anagrams provided for our amusement.

Unfortunately, because he set the story up the way he did, Brown can't let us in on the other theological joke associated with "Q." As any reasonably serious study of Christian history shows, the early Christian community testified to the existence of Matthew, Mark, Luke and John from the earliest times. Indeed, these Gospels were quoted so widely among early Christians that the individual quotes found in early Christian writings could be used to re-construct all four Gospels from scratch. It is now clear that the long period of time necessary for "Q" to evolve simply wasn't available – all four Gospels existed by the year 100 A.D. Thus, although it was popular in Germany in the early 1900's, and had some popularity in the United States in the middle of the 20th century, serious scholars reject "Q" theory today. Indeed, knowledgeable theologians refer to this theory not as the "Quelle" theory, but as the "Quatsch" theory. "Quatsch" is German for "rubbish."

MEROVINGIANS FOUNDED PARIS
CHAPTER 60, PAGE 257

Paris is over 2000 years old. If the Merovingians really descended from Jesus, and Jesus died only 2000 years ago, how did they manage this? In fact, Paris was founded by the Parisii, a band of Celts who settled the island in the third century B.C. It takes its name from them.

PLANTARD AND SAINT CLAIRE
CHAPTER 61, PAGE 260

It is not for nothing that one of Sophie's parents is named Plantard (Chapter 105, page 442). See the comments on Chapter 23, page 113.

NEKKUDOT
CHAPTER 71, PAGE 299

Written Hebrew has letters only for consonants, none for vowels. It also has no spacing between words. Thus, a book written in the Hebrew language would consist of a long string of consonants and nothing else. When Hebrews speak of the Word of God, they aren't kidding: in Hebrew, Scripture is literally one long word. The only way anyone can read it is to be taught by someone who knows where the vowels go. By the late 700's, a family of Jewish scribes finally got tired of dealing with a vowel-less language, and developed a system of vowel notation that they used in their copies of Scripture. The presence of vowel notation is what distinguishes a Masoretic text from other Hebrew texts. Nekkudot is the system of vowel notation. See the notes on Chapter 74, page 309: "Jehovah" for commentary on why this is important.

LA LINGUA PURA
CHAPTER 72, PAGE 303

In Langdon's universe, the Priory considers English the only European language "linguistically removed" from the Romance languages (French, Spanish and Italian) which all "were rooted in Latin."

This idea is, to say the least, a little odd. English is notorious for stealing words from every source imaginable. It has the largest vocabulary in the world, which is one of the reasons it works so well as an international language: it has words for every situation. If it doesn't, it steals some. It is chock-full of words whose origins are Latin, French, Italian and Spanish. Worse, English was hardly a secret language, rather, for most of the Middle Ages it was the language of the British farmer, while French or Latin was the language of the aristocracy.

If the members of the Priory wanted a European language that was relatively untouched by Latin, German would be the choice. It was the source from which English originally sprung. It is easily much more "pure" than English since it never acquired the baggage of words with Romance language derivations that English carries. Aristocracy recommends it: Emperor Charles V said, "I speak Spanish to God, Italian to women, French to men and German to my horse."

Finally, German fits much better with the philosophical underpinnings of goddess religion. As Anna Bramwell points out in *Ecology in the 20th Century: A History*, German national socialism was the only European fascist party to express concerns about the environment. This is not surprising. Germany has a long history of using nature as a philosophical guide. A strong ecological movement within Germany wanted to replace Christian traditions with Germanic nature myths. Germany, it was argued, had been forcibly ripped from her nature worship by the artificial imposition of Constantine's Christianity.

German scholars insisted that society was originally matriarchal, originally built around equality between the sexes, with women slightly superior. Furthermore, close ties existed between these German ecological societies and their English counterparts, the nudist colonies where Gerald Gardner's Wicca would flourish. Many of the leaders of the German ecological movement became early members of the Nazi party. English Darwinian theory tied tightly into this ascendancy of nature worship and formed a firm basis for German policy prior to and during the Second World War.

For further illustration of this theme, see the commentaries on "Shekinah as spiritual equal to God," Chapter 74, page 309, "'Q' theory," Chapter 60, page 256, "*Malleus Maleficorum*, The Hammer of Witches," Chapter 28, page 125, and "The chalice and the blade," Chapter 56, pages 237-239. An excellent book outlining German feminist theology is Manfred Hauke's *God or Goddess?*

GNOSIS IS FOR MAN, NOT FOR WOMAN
CHAPTER 74, PAGE 308

See the commentary on "Quoting the Gospel of Mary Magdalene" Chapter 58, page 247. Langdon has things exactly backward.

SHEKINAH AS SPIRITUAL EQUAL TO GOD
CHAPTER 74, PAGE 309

Langdon says Constantine commissioned a new Bible in order to correct the New Testament, but now we see he must have commissioned a new Old Testament as well. After all, the Old Testament absolutely forbids the kind of activity Langdon claims occurred in the Temple. Orgiastic activity in or near the Temple took place only when the Jews had fallen away from the Faith, rejected God and returned to pagan apostasy. Though this book has so far shown exactly how impeccably thorough Dan Brown's scholarship is, the reasons for this erroneous description of the Shekinah from Langdon may go deeper than even Mr. Brown realizes.

In the commentary on Chapter 60, page 256, the origin of the "Q" theory and its basis in attacking Catholic Faith was discussed. However, there was another set of theories that were designed to attack another segment of the population. The JEPD theory and form criticism, called "the higher criticism," attacked what the Christians called the Old Testament, and what the Jews called the Law and the Prophets.

In this theory, German scholars attempted to destroy the validity of the Old Testament by questioning the authorship of the Pentateuch and the prophets, using exactly the same kind of logic they had used with "Q." The Pentateuch especially came under attack, and it was asserted that at least four different communities contributed to the work: a group who preferred the word "Yahweh" (J group), the "Elohists" who preferred to use the word "Elohim" (E group), the Priestly community (P group) and the Deuteronomists (D group). All prophetic elements in the Hebrew Scriptures are explicitly denied. Anytime a prophecy of Scripture appears to have come true, the scholars use this accurate prediction as evidence that the book in question must have been written *after* the event that was prophesied. After all, how could anyone accurately predict the future?

These scholars denied Hebrew prophets had even the normal human powers of prediction available to anyone who keeps vague track of world affairs. After all, it took no great skill for the men and the woman of the 1930's to predict that war would soon break out in Europe. Similarly, once five carrier groups assembled in the vicinity of Saddam Hussein's Iraq, predicting the American invasion was rather easy. But even this level of prediction is essentially denied to the Hebrew prophets – they are too stupid to do anything but write down events that had already happened and then pretend the events were prophesied.

In order to make this theory work, the scholars also had to give short shrift to all the warnings in Scripture against liars. Of all the sins that can be committed, the warning against the lying heart and the lying tongue are the most prevalent in the Law and the Prophets. Honesty is among the most highly prized of Jewish virtues. But, by proposing JEPD and related theories, 19th century German scholars essentially asserted the Hebrew prophets were both stupid and liars.

Germans had their reasons. By denying all the prophetic elements of Jewish Scripture and repudiating the widely accepted authorship of the various books, German scholars in the years leading up to World War I cast doubt on the validity of both Jewish and Catholic faith, preparing for the ascendancy of nature worship and attempting to consolidate Bismark's *Kulturkampf*. Orthodox Jews called this Germanic attempt to destroy the authority of their prophets and their sacred books "the higher anti-semitism." In light of this history, and the level of scholarship Dan Brown is known to have undertaken, Langdon's comments raise interesting questions about the philosophical basis of goddess worship.

DERIVATION OF THE WORD "JEHOVAH"
CHAPTER 74, PAGE 309

In Langdon's universe, what he says here might be true. In ours, it is complete balderdash. The word Jehovah is the result of a translation error by "scholars" who didn't know Hebrew very well. As is noted in the commentary on "Nekkudot," Chapter 71, page 299, written Hebrew has no vowels. The vowel markings developed long after written Hebrew was developed. This forms the basis for the problem.

In Hebrew, the word for God is "Yahweh", but it is considered too sacred to speak aloud. It is written JHWH. In public recitation, another word, "Adonai," which means "Lord," was substituted for it. Since the scrolls were read aloud, the Hebrew copyists had to have some way of maintaining the word JHWH, while notifying the reader that he should substitute "Adonai" if he were reading it aloud. The solution was ingenious. The consonants were kept: JHWH, but instead of using the vowel markings for JHWH, the vowel markings for either "Adonai" or "Elohim" were used. When the reader encountered this nonsense word that looked vaguely like Yahweh, but had all the wrong vowels, he would instantly recall, "Oh yes. I'm supposed to say 'Adonai' here."

However, if the resulting mish-mash of consonants and vowels were directly translated, the result would literally be "Jahovah" or "Jehovah." No rabbinically-trained student of Hebrew would make that translation mistake, since his rabbi instructor would certainly inform the student of the reason for the vowel substitution. Unfortunately, not everyone who learned Hebrew was trained by rabbis. Apparently, some Christians either got initial instruction from a rabbi, but then continued study on their own, or they taught themselves Hebrew without benefit of rabbinic instruction at all.

As a result, they fell into this fairly silly translation error. The earliest known example of it comes in the early 1500's. As acquaintance with the ancient languages became more common in the 19th century, the error became more widespread. It has been most popular among Christian denominations whose leaders do not have much or any formal language training: one excellent example of such a group is the aptly mis-named Jehovah's Witnesses. See the previous comments on "Shekinah" for more information.

DESCRIPTION OF THE RITUAL
CHAPTER 74, PAGES 310-311

Dan Brown claims all rituals are accurately described. One can only ask how he knows this. But, beyond that, it is interesting to note the incipient appeal made to his largely female audience here. Men, being more visually oriented, tend to focus more on the visual and physical pleasures of sex. Women, on the other hand, generally focus more on the unitive aspect of the act. By putting a woman who is "plump, far from perfect" in the ritual sex ceremony and speaking about it as a mystical experience, he appeals directly to his female readership.

Of course, the same appealing aura couldn't be made with a description of the ritual spanking initiation which Wicca often requires, so that particular description is left entirely out of the novel, as is the fact that Wicca was created to slake one man's adulterous desires. See the notes on "Relics and Wicca," Chapter 4, page 23.

BAPHOMET
CHAPTER 76, PAGE 316

See "The Knights Templar," Chapter 38, page 159. Of the literally hundreds of charges King Philip levelled against the knights, only one of the knights was accused of worshipping Baphomet.

"FAITH IS BASED ON FABRICATION"
CHAPTER 82, PAGE 341

This is, of course, a complete misrepresentation of faith. A simple example would suffice to demonstrate the fact. Let us assume that you are a close personal friend of mine living in a distant city. I drive over to visit you. While at your house, my car breaks down. I know nothing about the mechanics in this town, so I ask your advice. You tell me to go to a certain mechanic. I do. That is faith.

Faith is not a fabrication. Faith is based on evidence. I know you are my friend, I know you do not intend me to be cheated. My evidence for this knowledge is our past relationship with one another – our shared experiences, our dangers endured together, our laughs enjoyed together. Since I know you from long association together, I have perfect confidence that you have sent me to the best mechanic you know.

Now, have I seen the mechanic work? Of course not. Do I know he is good? Not personally, no. My faith in you is the evidence of things seen, my faith in him is the evidence of things not seen. But my faith in him comes from my faith in you. Are you a fabrication? No, you are most assuredly not. That's precisely why I can trust you, why I can have faith. If you were a fabrication, I couldn't have faith in you or in the mechanic your fabricated person recommended.

To "prove" something means to test it. That's why experimental weapons are sent to "proving" grounds. Faith is most definitely something that we prove every day, something we test constantly. I have faith in my own judgement and in yours, but every day, these faiths get tested, proved, against reality. Every day I have to judge whether or not I can continue to have faith in my judgement and your friendship. Faith in God is much the same thing.

God has demonstrated His love for us by giving us a world that is quite useful and rich. He gives us a long history of His association with a specific people, people who were not at all kind or faithful towards Him. Yet He remained faithful, despite everything we did to Him. He has been our support through thick and thin. In fact, He entered creation just to take on the pain we ourselves had generated, heal the world we broke. He did this to free us. We test Him constantly, and He has always come through.

This is the source of Faith in God. We look at the history of His interaction with mankind. We look at the way we betrayed Him and ourselves and how He answered those constant betrayals, and we decide. Is He worthy of our trust? We can now see that Faith has two components: Faith is the evidence a person reveals to us about himself through constant interaction with the persons around him. Faith is also the power to recognize the consistency of the other person's character. Faith is both the content of evidence and the power to recognize the consistent truth towards which the evidence points. Both are necessary.

That's why Faith and Reason support each other, and neither can be dispensed with. Reason is an aspect of Faith, it is part of the fuel, the power we need to recognize where the evidence is pointing. See "Bishop Aringarosa is a fideist," Chapter 34, page 149.

WHY THE TEMPLE CHURCH IS ROUND
CHAPTER 83, PAGE 343

It was round to honor the Church of the Holy Sepulchre, which was destroyed by the Muslims in 1009. See the notes on "Acts of war against the enemies of God had been committed for centuries. Forgiveness was assured," Chapter 2, page 13.

TROUBADOUR MINISTERS
CHAPTER 95, PAGE 390

A fascinating conjecture, but no evidence is provided in the novel to support the contention, nor does any evidence in the history of our universe exist to support it. See "Leonardo's "documented" goddess worship," Chapter 20, page 96.

NEWTON'S SCIENCE INCURRED CHURCH WRATH
CHAPTER 95, PAGE 392

Here's a puzzler. What is Langdon talking about? He couldn't be referring to Galileo, because Galileo was dead before Newton was born. Newton built on Galileo's work, not the other way around.

Even if Galileo was born after Newton in Langdon's universe, Langdon would still be wrong. Any decent investigation into the trial of Galileo demonstrates that Galileo was set up for a fall by university academics. Galileo underwent two trials, twenty years apart. After the first trial, he was exonerated, but his academic enemies introduced false evidence into his trial record after the fact. Twenty years later, when the second trial was convened, nearly everyone who had been involved in the first trial was dead, except for the Pope himself, who could not follow trial details due to foreign emergencies. The judges at the second trial saw the forged evidence, didn't realize it was forged, and on the basis of this evidence, pronounced Galileo "vehemently suspected of heresy." Even Thomas Huxley, the man who invented the word "agnostic" and who was so dogged in his attacks on religion and his support of evolution that he was called "Darwin's bulldog," admitted that the Galileo affair was not the fault of the Catholic Church.

There simply aren't any other instances of the Church getting involved in science. Certainly there is no hint of Catholic involvement or rancor at Newton's science or at the discoveries in physics that depend on his work. Newton was a mathematician and physicist. The last physicist who got in trouble with the Church was Galileo, and that was an academic setup.

OPUS DEI TO BECOME "A CHURCH UNTO ITSELF"
CHAPTER 100, PAGE 415

As the book began with weird terminology from the mouths of Catholic bishops, so it ends with weird terminology from the mouths of Catholic bishops. As was pointed out in the commentary on Chapter 5, page 29, no Catholic organization talks about being "a church" in the Catholic Church. That is strictly evangelical Christian terminology. In fact, the terminology in this conversation is so odd that it is difficult for Catholics to figure out what the conversation is about. Apparently, Brown's plot calls for Opus Dei to be put into schism by the hierarchy in Rome. This is supposed to be the driving motive for the whole book's events. But that's absurd. It is exactly what Rome would never do.

Rome never drives schism. She does everything she can do to *prevent* schism. Berengarius, one of the first men to deny the Real Presence of Christ in the Eucharist around 1000 A.D., was given ten years to recant. Luther was likewise given years to recant. Blatant heretics are always given years to recant, and less blatant heretics are generally left pretty much alone. Schisms take forever to heal, and Rome isn't interested in having more schisms than is absolutely necessary.

Worse, this isn't just a single heretic or group of heretics. Rather, Opus Dei is akin to an entire order within the Church. Rome would never create schism over this kind of organization: there's no need. She can simply suppress it. Though rare, there are a very few cases in which Rome suppressed an entire order, most notably the Jesuits. But even this took an enormous amount of petitioning from all the crowned heads of Europe to accomplish the deed, and the Jesuit order was re-constituted within a century.

If Opus Dei or any similar organization or order became a serious problem, Rome would suppress it; she would not demand that the organization become schismatic. But the characters in the book who are supposed to be members of the Roman Curia aren't telling Opus Dei about an impending suppression of the order, which would be plausible. Instead the hierarchy seems intent on creating a schism, which is absurd.

SILAS IMPERSONATES A PRIEST
CHAPTER 101, PAGE 421

Impersonating a priest for the purposes of misleading someone else is a mortal sin. Even assuming that finding the keystone was good (an arguable proposition), no pious Catholic is permitted to do evil that good may come of it. So, as Silas searched for the keystone, he commits two mortal sins with a single statement: he pretended to be a priest breaking the seal of the confessional, and he lied. Any authority on Catholicism knows no priest would ever break the seal of the confessional – it is automatic excommunication. In the sacrament of reconciliation, Christ casts our sins as far as east is from west. Only Satan would insist on dwelling on sins God has forgiven. Why would the art museum director, a supposed expert on Catholic faith and discipline, fall for such a patent absurdity? That, like nearly every other seemingly factual statement in the book, is not explained.

If you would like to see an *excellent* movie that shows the seal of the confessional in action, rent Alfred Hitchcock's *I Confess*. Invite a priest. They sweat bullets when they watch it.

CONCLUSION

The strangest omission in a book that purports to be about goddesses is that of the Blessed Virgin Mary. She is mentioned once in passing, as a symbol that supposedly hearkens back to Egyptian goddesses. But certainly her presence in nearly every portrait of the infant Christ would seem to merit her more mention than that? Wouldn't you think Mary Magdalene's mother-in-law would be worthy of discussion in a book about the sacred feminine? Apparently not.

If this novel were in any sense pretending to be an accurate history, we would have to conclude many unfavorable things about Dan Brown. Did the author seriously intend to present Catholic Faith accurately? If so, how can he justify these mistakes? Worse, if he can't get the Catholic Faith right when its practitioners are everywhere and accurate documentation on it is abundant, on what grounds should we believe *any* of his "historical" research concerning pagan goddesses is correct? After all, information on goddesses and their cults is not nearly as easy to come by as information on the Catholic Church, yet the information on the latter is consistently wrong. No wonder he thinks faith is a fabrication.

Non-Catholic Christians of various stripes have, over the years, accused the Church of making Mary out to be a goddess. When the doctrine of the Co-Redemptrix redeemed an otherwise slow news summer a few years back, either Time or Newsweek (they are pretty much interchangeable) ran a cover story about Mary being elevated to the fourth Person of the Trinity. We should applaud Dan Brown for at least this much acumen: he has more sense and subtlety than most journalists. At least he didn't do that.

In the end, *The Da Vinci Code* is built on a single principle, enunciated by Langdon near the beginning of the book: "Misunderstanding breeds distrust." Everything the novel intends us to distrust is crowded around with misunderstandings, misstatements and mistakes. Given that his own character consciously enunciates the principle, we can only assume Dan Brown consciously intended to use the method to discredit Opus Dei and the Catholic Church.

Spend more than a moment thinking about the plot and it all dissolves into nonsense. It simply says this: *if* Jesus was married, *then* we should worship goddesses by having ritual sex in front of admiring crowds. The leap from the premise to the conclusion is enormous, but that is essentially the author's argument. Even if Mr. Brown's Holy Grail legend were perfectly accurate, it would make Sophie and her brother nothing more than Jewish royalty. A sensible plot would have them go to Jerusaelm to be crowned and take over the government. Instead, Sophie is... what exactly? Nobody knows.

After two thousand years, it has all become rather boring. There are a limited number of ways to misrepresent Church teaching, and by this time, pretty much all of them have been tried and found wanting. Dan Brown has not brought forward a single new thought, a single new heresy. Nothing appears in his book that hasn't been thoroughly refuted a hundred times before in the twenty centuries prior to this moment. The only difference between Mr. Brown and earlier groups is he has made more money from it than they did. Such is the price of progress.

Whenever you see something that sounds vaguely unsettling, something that seems to undermine what the Church has always taught, remember this: there are no new heresies. Refuting them is just a matter of doing a little research and then giving your findings a little publicity, that's all.